InSites Consulting

First published in Belgium in 2013 by InSites Consulting.

Apart from any fair dealing for the purposes of research or private study, or criticism or review, as permitted under the Copyright, Designs and Patent Act 1988, this publication may only be reproduced, stored or transmitted, in any form or by any means, with the prior permission in writing of the publishers, or in the case of reprographic reproduction in accordance with the terms and licenses issued by the CLA. Enquiries concerning reproduction outside these terms should be send to the publishers at the undermentioned address:

Evergemsesteenweg 195

9032 Ghent

Belgium

www.insites-consulting.com

© InSites Consulting, 2013

The right of InSites Consulting to be identified as the author of this work has been asserted by the company in accordance with Copyright, Designs and Patent Act 1988.

ISBN 978 9 0820 5660 0

The
CONSUMER CONSULTING BOARD

Consumers shaping your business

'I periodically leave one seat open at a conference table and inform attendees that they should consider that seat to be occupied by their customer, the most important person in the room.'

**Jeff Bezos,
CEO Amazon**

'Put customers in the driver's seat, or be dead by 2020.'

**Jamie Nordstrom,
EVP Nordstrom**

'The era of consumer hierarchy is upon us.'

**Brian Solis,
Principal at Altimeter Group**

'The future requires brands to give control to consumers.'

**Pierre Woreczek,
Chief Brand & Strategy Office
McDonald's Europe**

'The consumer isn't a moron; she's your wife.'

**David Ogilvy,
Founder Ogilvy & Mather**

'Many old-school CEOs are
stuck in their ways;
we need more collaboration
and openness.'

**Paul Polman,
CEO Unilever**

'99.99% of the world's
smartest people don't work
for us.'

**Stiven Kerestegian,
Senior Manager Open Innovation
LEGO**

'The power of everyday
people is driving
monumental change.'

**Marc Pritchard,
CMO P&G**

'Step in the shoes of your
consumer and build new
relevance from that.'

**Alain Coumont,
Founder & CEO Le Pain Quotidien**

'Above all else, align with
customers. Win when they win.
Win only when they win.'

**Jeff Bezos,
CEO Amazon**

Foreword

I do an awful lot of work on a variety of fronts to understand how things are evolving between marketing and insights professionals. As an observer of the insights space, there is no greater barometer of how things are developing than talking to the key stakeholders involved and working with them collaboratively to help co-create solutions. In a sense, I consider the research industry an über-community and engage with them using many different tools to understand, engage, solve problems and deliver a fair value exchange for all parties for the effort.

That is why I have profound respect for the pioneering work being done in the community provider sector, and InSites Consulting is one of the handful of leaders that I pay attention to the most. They take the same principles and apply it to their business: connecting brands and key stakeholders for mutual benefit via the rubric of communities.

What is more, they also get the power of sharing learnings to empower everyone, and that brings us to this great book. The InSites Consulting team has put together a fantastic synthesis of their hard-won experience, best practices, wisdom and vision to help raise the game of everyone in the insights space: clients and suppliers (including their competitors!). Kudos to them for leading the charge in transforming the insights

space through transparency and knowledge sharing!

Through this book we get an interesting peek at how marketing and insights involving communities can bolster an organization. For those who are willing to dip their marketing toes into the insights pool, the benefits far outweigh any hesitation. For some marketers, something as simple as partnering with key constituents via the community process has helped focus marketing strategies. Others have seen substantial growth in client engagement and interactions just from sharing with their constituents via communities.

The conclusion? Bringing together those with solid ideas and those with a strong understanding of insights tools is simply the right thing to do. And InSites Consulting certainly gets that too. A strong message contained here (which is validated by my own experience and the sky-rocketing growth of providers in this space due to client adoption of the community model) is for those using communities, it clearly has proven to be worth the time and investment. For some, this tool has helped reach the right customer at the right time. As one client stated in the recent GRIT report: 'It provides us with a barometer of when people are engaging, what they are engaging with and what is driving the business.'

Communities are a wonderful tool for supporting brand initiatives. Yes, it

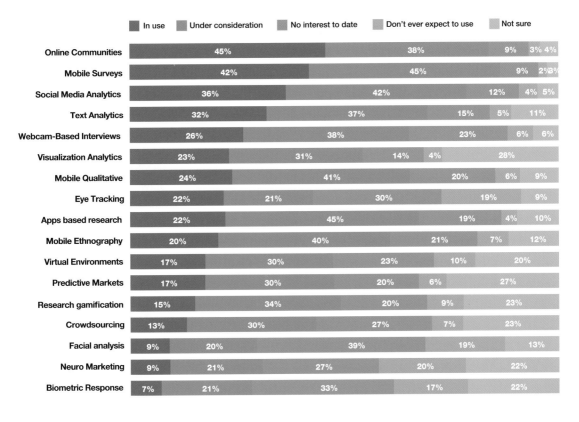

	In use	Under consideration	No interest to date	Don't ever expect to use	Not sure
Online Communities	45%	38%	9%	3%	4%
Mobile Surveys	42%	45%	9%	2%	3%
Social Media Analytics	36%	42%	12%	4%	5%
Text Analytics	32%	37%	15%	5%	11%
Webcam-Based Interviews	26%	38%	23%	6%	6%
Visualization Analytics	23%	31%	14%	4%	28%
Mobile Qualitative	24%	41%	20%	6%	9%
Eye Tracking	22%	21%	30%	19%	9%
Apps based research	22%	45%	19%	4%	10%
Mobile Ethnography	20%	40%	21%	7%	12%
Virtual Environments	17%	30%	23%	10%	20%
Predictive Markets	17%	30%	20%	6%	27%
Research gamification	15%	34%	20%	9%	23%
Crowdsourcing	13%	30%	27%	7%	23%
Facial analysis	9%	20%	39%	19%	13%
Neuro Marketing	9%	21%	27%	20%	22%
Biometric Response	7%	21%	33%	17%	22%

works for measuring attitudes and impressions of your brand. However, some have taken it one step further by using information derived from their communities to transform the perception of their brand among those who engage with it online. And, to answer the eternal ROI question, some said the real benefit to the process was the ability to prove the value and demonstrate the effectiveness of their efforts. Additional benefits of using online research communities collected in the GRIT data included user-friendliness, customization and the fact that they provide a way to keep a finger on the pulse of customers' needs and attitudes.

....

'Provides continuous feedback in a cost-effective manner.'

'Quick and easy access.'

'They're economical and provide the information we are looking for.'

Extracts from the GRIT Report

....

THE WORLD is changing

creating new products or services that will drive target customer engagement and spending.

- Data alone does not deliver insight; it informs it. Insight is supported and driven by a variety of factors, but ultimately it is people who uncover insights and develop winning strategies based on them.

- Client organizations are not experts in insights; they are experts in their business. They need multi-disciplinary partners to help them get to the point in the process where their business expertize can be applied to the insight process.

- Supplier partners that can help client organizations understand, engage and deliver value to customers through the insight process win business and grow.

Communities (and all the various approaches they enable) help meet that need for clients in an instantly globally scalable way. It is the type of integrated offering they have been clamoring for but has not been fully delivered on by other techniques such as surveys, focus groups or even social media and big data analytics. The community is rapidly becoming the hub of the insights wheel.

Consider this quote from **Marc Pritchard**, Global Marketing and Brand Building Officer of **P&G** regarding the company's view on how technology is changing the game for them:

Many of you reading this may still struggle to see how to implement these techniques into your current programs and worry about customers' reactions to being engaged in these ways. All I can say is that the window for community usage being a choice is rapidly shrinking.

First, let's look at things from a strictly business strategy standpoint:

- In an increasingly competitive and complex marketing climate, more and more clients are looking to the insight function to help fuel competitive advantage.

- Competitive advantage often is focused on the front end of innovation;

'To address these technology forces, our vision is to build our brands through lifelong, one-to-one relationships in real time with every person in the world. The power of everyday people is driving monumental change and people power favors brands like ours. We have trusted brands that are part of everyday life. We genuinely care about serving people with superior benefits and doing good. Technology will mean that people will increasingly expect brands to understand their unique needs and deliver. We want P&G to be the first to create this trusted, indispensable relationship because it will create greater loyalty, more purchases across categories, and more sales at lower costs. Achieving this vision requires some fundamental shifts in how we operate.'

It is a perfect validation for why the growth of a community-driven insight model, especially one that is focused on co-creation, is perfect for the new age of socialized branding.

Consider this your guide book to get started on building an insight organization that will support the development of a one-to-one relationship with your key constituents. The value of the effort is proven, but the potential is far from fulfilled (yet). The InSites Consulting team have done a fabulous job here of showing us the power of communities and firing the imagination on where we may get to as this model takes its rightful place as the core driver of the insight function.

Leonard Murphy
Editor-in-chief at GreenBook Blog

🐦 @lennyism
in linkedin.com/in/leonardfmurphy

Leonard (Lenny) Murphy is a seasoned and respected industry leader with an entrepreneurial drive. He is a visionary entrepreneur and innovator, and has successfully established several companies in the market research space including Rockhopper Research, a leading full service global research firm and MDM Associates, a market research consulting firm, before founding his current company, BrandScan 360. Mr. Murphy is a key consultant and advisor to numerous market research agencies, and works across the industry to drive the development of innovative research practices by developing strategic alliances with multiple *best in class* providers. Lenny serves on the Board of The Market Research Global Alliance, the premier social network for the global market research profession. He is the Founder and Executive Director of the Research Industry Trends Monitoring Group & Publisher of the Research Industry Trends Study, the oldest study in the industry devoted to tracking changing trends in research. Rounding out his busy professional life, he is the Editor in Chief of the GreenBook Blog.

Introduction

Back in 2006, we ran our very first community. It made us a true pioneer of what has now become one of the most popular ways to listen to, understand and collaborate with consumers. Research communities are probably the fastest growing research methodology ever. According to the latest *GRIT* study,[1] 45% of the research market appeals to communities and another 38% is currently developing them for the first time. This is causing a fundamental shift in the way research is done: from treating participants as a resource to using them as a source of inspiration, from just asking questions to collaboration and from running ad hoc projects to having a more ongoing dialogue with the consumer world.

In 2011, we coined the term *Consumer Consulting Board* © for the first time; it is probably a better name to indicate how we manage research communities and the position we give them within a company. It indicates that if you run them well, communities allow you to make use of the consulting power of consumers - both current and potential users of a product or service: they will help you make more consumer-relevant decisions. Moreover, the name embodies that companies need to see and treat their consumer community as a board of advisors they rely on almost every single day, for most business decisions taken across the different departments of the company. In that sense, it is more than just another market research tool. A Consumer Consulting Board gives you the strategic capability to (re)shape your business together with consumers.

Today, InSites Consulting builds and manages over 150 Consumer Consulting Boards a year, for the world's biggest brands. In the past 7 years we facilitated over 600,000 conversations. And with our 5 offices and moderation teams in more than 30 countries, we are connecting companies with their consumers worldwide, providing them with the unique capability to make better business decisions faster and to turn their organizations into consumer-centric thinking ones.

We are proud to present this new book to you. It is the fruit of years of work in the field of Consumer Consulting Boards by the entire InSites Consulting team. We have a tradition of sharing our knowledge with the world through publications and conference talks around the globe. This book gives an overview of our collective wisdom in the domain of communities, based on research-on-research by our *ForwaR&D Lab* (our very own innovation center), more than 40 articles and papers we have published and presented at conferences, our ongoing dialogue with research community members in our *Walk the Talk* community, co-creation sessions with our moderators around the world, collaborations with academic institutions and brainstorms and business projects with clients in a wide range of industries among different cultures. It is that overview of our findings and wide global experience that we will share with you.

In the true spirit of co-creation the book has been developed jointly by 14 different contributors who give an insight into their knowledge, our best practices and results from client projects. A brief overview of the 5 chapters:

1. Chapter one investigates what people expect from brands today and how organizations can make use of social channels, tools and platforms to co-create and structurally collaborate with the consumer world. The world has changed: how to adapt, survive and win in the era of the empowered consumer?

2. In the second chapter we unveil our secret recipe behind successfully setting up, managing and getting the most out of Consumer Consulting Boards. We share our strategy to communicate research results in an impactful way and tell you all about how to embed structural collaboration with consumers within the business.

3. Chapter three talks about Consumer Consulting Boards in action. It introduces the different issues companies encounter these days and describes how consumers help solving them. Our findings are illustrated with the visions of senior

executives of leading brands and a selection of projects we conducted for our clients.

4. The main subjects of chapter four are: what does it take to run communities in different cultures and how should your brand be adapted to the new reality of globalization, a shift in economic power and Gen Y as the most influential generation ever. It is an introduction to the brave new world we are living in.

5. In the final chapter, we take a closer look at what societal trends and evolutions within marketing and research tell us about the future of Consumer Consulting Boards. We also give an insight in how we collaborate with our key stakeholders (clients, participants and members) to already create that future today.

13

Many people make a publication like this a success. A special thank you to our fellow authors, contributors and reviewers (**Niels Schillewaert**, **Annelies Verhaeghe**, **Thomas Troch**, **Anouk Willems**, **Natalie Mas**, **Joeri Van den Bergh**, **Anneleen Boullart**, **Liesbeth Dambre**, **Els Cocquyt**, **Wim De Wever**, **Oana Frentiu**, **Alexandra Ardean**, **Hakim Zemni**, **Stijn Poffé**, **Sorina Badau**, **Liana Sentici**, **Pieter van Remortel**, **Anne-Laure Simoens** and **Ashley Smith**), to **Lenny Murphy** for writing the preface, to the entire InSites Consulting team for 7 years of great work, to **Stephan Ludwig** (who

The InSites Consulting team

spent 4 years of his life on understanding communities during his PhD sponsored by InSites Consulting), to **Dado Van Peteghem** (moderator of our very first community), to **Elias Veris**, **Steven Van Belleghem**, all the academic institutions we worked with over the years (the **universities of Maastricht, Wageningen** and **Nijmegen**, the **IESEG School of Management, Lille,** and the **Vlerick Business School**), the research and marketing associations who stimulate us to share our expertise with the rest of the industry (**ESOMAR**, **MRS**, **AMA**, **CASRO**, **MRA**, **MOA**, **BAQMaR**, **ARF** and **Febelmar**), the domain experts and CxOs we interviewed for this book and to all our clients and the moderators and members of the Consumer Consulting Boards. And last but not least, to **Anke**

Moerdyck for coordinating the whole creation process of this book together with **Natalie Mas**. **Hannes Willaert** and **Karl Demoen** for making our pieces look great by their graphic design and our families for supporting us every single day in living our passion for helping companies to get the most out of the voice of the consumer.

We hope this book will inspire you to make a start with structural collaboration or that it will offer you fresh insights in order to continue your path towards becoming an *open*, *agile* and *consumer-centric thinking* company. It is time to get to the future… first!

Enjoy your read and we are looking forward to your feedback, thoughts and ideas.

Tom De Ruyck
Head of Consumer
Consulting Boards
InSites Consulting

🐦 *@tomderuyck*

Kristof De Wulf
CEO and Co-Founder
InSites Consulting

🐦 *@kristofdewulf*

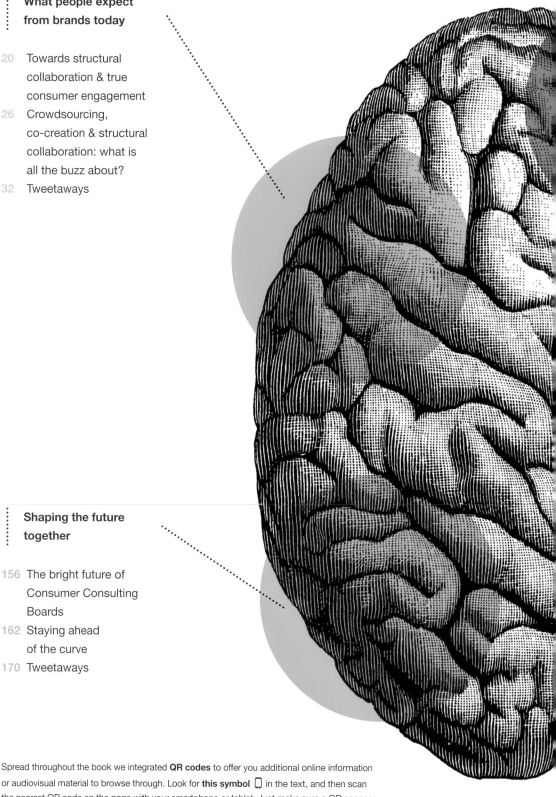

Spread throughout the book we integrated **QR codes** to offer you additional online information or audiovisual material to browse through. Look for **this symbol** ☐ in the text, and then scan the nearest QR code on the page with your smartphone or tablet. Just make sure a QR scanner application is downloaded on your smartphone/tablet.

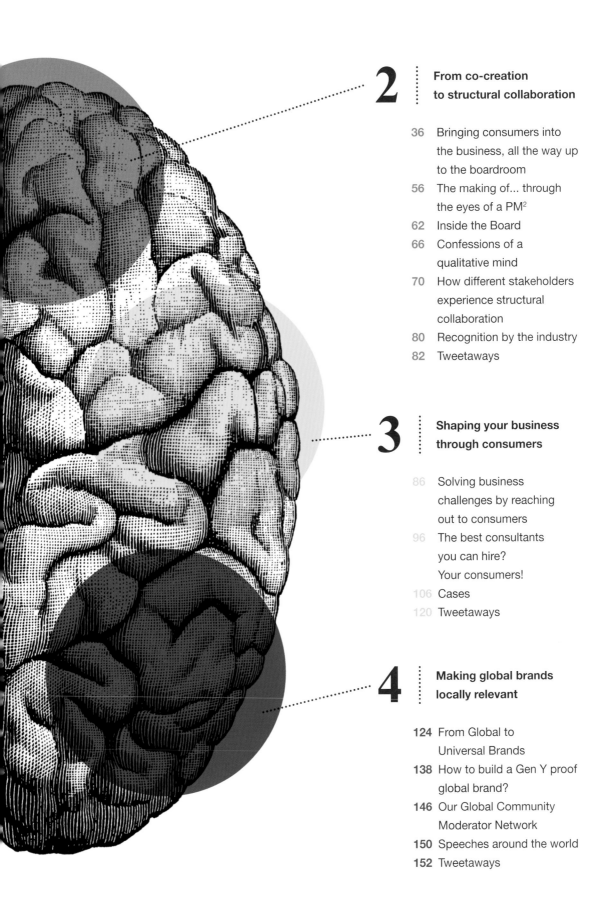

What people expect from brands today

Towards
structural collaboration &
true consumer engagement

by Niels Schillewaert

Through instead of *to* consumers

In the nineties marketers were in control. All eyes were focused on effective targeting via 1-on-1 techniques, direct and database marketing strategies. Now, everything has changed. Technological innovation has led where marketing attention has followed and consumers have obtained a place in the driver's seat more than ever before. The surge of social media has been a major driving force behind consumers gaining power versus brands. Related behaviors (as a result or cause) such as participation, information contribution and sharing, social networking, brand liking, product reviewing, user collaboration and co-creation… have become the new norm when it comes to consumer behavior.

Marketing anno 2013 has evolved from a dominantly *to consumers* approach to a *through consumers* approach. Gradually, we see marketing move up to work together with consumers, to collaborate with them, to achieve goals through them. The days are gone where we send out a message and want people to react. Marketers need to rely on consumers doing things for brands because they love to do so. Today we want consumers to want to participate in our brand activation. The unilateral call to action no longer works, the call to collaboration is inevitable. Many consumer trends show that companies have no choice but to adapt to this reality.[1]

Human brands with a purpose

Consumers want brands that behave humanly and have a higher purpose. Brands should show they care and admit their flaws. **Patagonia** for example shows that good P&L can be combined with serving a bigger cause. The high-end outdoor clothing company is embraced by consumers because of its continued humility, empathy and generosity in minimizing the environmental cost of clothing. Patagonia allows consumers to have clothing repaired at nominal cost, the brand facilitates donating used clothing to charity or selling it on **eBay**'s *Common Thread* site. Even more extremely, the brand advertised to consumers on *Black Friday* not to buy their clothes because it takes a lot of resources to make them. Stimulating people NOT to consume as much on the world's biggest buying day or to at least think about it, is quite remarkable. Another example is **Domino**'s *2011 billboard Twitter campaign*. The fast food retailer hired a billboard on Times Square which live-streamed consumer feedback, good or bad. Always a risk, but consumers appreciate it.

Social status through deal making

Consumers like to have a sense of mastery in finding that best price, price-quality or even luxury deal for whatever need they wish to fulfill. It is a new sense of accomplishment for consumers if they capture the best deal and get the recognition of their peers for it.

Groupon is probably the most well-known business model of the *dealer-chic* trend as consumers work together to achieve a specific deal. Other examples are music-sharing services such as **Songza** or **Grooveshark**. Finding that unique playlist that makes an impression on friends is what people value. Or just think about how we travel. Everyone is a travel agent these days. Traveling with friends and family is often partly *do it yourself* and being able to come up with a nice gem or offer is well received and provides social status to the finder.

Distributed everything

This refers to the fact that value creation also becomes more widely distributed. With easy-to-use technologies in the hands of *amateur consumers*, they are capable of delivering content up to professional standards or capture unique information in the heat of the moment. Marketers should ask themselves what cannot be distributed (not what can) in their process delivery and focus on that. The ☐ **Heineken** *Open Design Explorations* initiative invited clubbers and up-and-coming designers to create the club of the future. Consumers identified needs and frictions throughout the clubbing journey which designers then leveraged to design the club of the future.

Social and mobile omnipresent

The new screen culture of consumers implies that consumers' media attention and shopping spending go social

Heineken Open Design Explorations Edition 1: The Club

and mobile. Consumers constantly tweet and update their status and feelings while watching TV. The new-age smartphone users use their phone for (peer-to-peer) payments, barcodes or couponing. It implies marketers have to be present everywhere and combine media to convince more than ever before.

Brands demanding consumers to act

But if done well, brands may swing the other way and become meaningfully demanding towards consumers too. If consumers believe the bigger vision of the brand, they will contribute and collaborate automatically. The Swedish charity newspaper **Faktum** has launched a social awareness campaign *Faktum Hotels* in Gothenburg. The campaign wants to bring the homeless problem to people's attention and encourages people to experience or gift a homeless night to a friend by means of a hotel-like website with hard-hitting scenes and pictures. Faktum's request is sizeable, but the story so compelling and humanized that consumers go the extra mile.

While all of these trends are real and social media have played a big role in their emergence, marketers are still using scoial media in a dominantly uni-dimensional, traditional and opportunistic way. They have mainly focused on large scale reach. Generating reach is easy and can be bought, but the real value lies in creating true engagement

Faktum Hotels website

and brand intimacy with people. Usually this grows organically. Consumers generate more information faster than ever before as well as better and more complete information, due to the fact that they have their own media at their fingertips. By using mobile devices and electronics, consumers generate contextual information that is illustrative and generated during the actual experience. Still, very few companies have understood that information and value streams should go *through* consumers rather than *to* them. Many companies only think about building as many fans and likes on Facebook as possible, not about mutual quality connections. Many overly focus on social media listening and social CRM because they want to control; brands do not focus on understanding, let alone they show empathy. A recent study from NetBase[2] shows that, while consumers want companies to listen in, the former want it to

23

happen on the consumers own terms. Consumers do not want companies to listen in a top-down manner such that it serves the sole commercial benefit of companies.

Another example of the demonstration that marketers do not get the new model yet is the recent debate on **Coca-Cola** revealing that a study of theirs did not show a correlation between social buzz and short-term sales.[3] Of course there is no correlation from a general perspective. We can come up with a number of statistical as well as conceptual reasons for why there is not, but it also does not at all mean social media are not valuable. For example, consumers like a brand they buy and consume all the time at different points in time. When people *like* a brand it does not imply

the same thing (it could mean more or less) as actually buying or adoring the brand. And they were probably buying it anyway, so adding *likes* did not do anything directly related to sales. The discussion also should not be about a single medium. Earned, paid, owned, online as well as offline media are all playing together in combination - it is hard to disentangle. Perhaps more importantly, what this discussion shows is the narrow-minded focus of marketers today. The real success for Coca-Cola is in brand building, whether that is through online or offline media; it should really be via social in the true sense of the word. Therefore, marketers need to understand what makes people really identify, love and engage with a brand. So what does all this imply for marketing research? That is what this book is all about - it is about *humans* and *relationships*. It is not about technology or panels but about how we can leverage consumers to reveal the information and knowledge we want to get at. Anything we do should be a positive brand touch-point experience for consumers and executives. People do not pay attention to boring things, so it is time to rethink research from that perspective. Far and foremost, we need to create internal impact among executives and make sure that research becomes a conversation starter within companies.

We need to realize that people need a good reason to participate in research or pay attention to its results. The only thing marketers, researchers and brands can and should do is facilitate human connections in a relevant way. Consumers are interested in doing things with other

Social Media around the World study

people. The new role of marketing and research is to provide social currency to consumers such that they can spend time together and do what they love to do. Our own ☐ *Social Media around the World study* confirms this from a consumer standpoint. Over 8 out of 10 consumers want to help in co-creation projects for brands and companies they like. Their preferred way of doing so is through a form of structural collaboration such as Consumer Consulting Boards or market research online communities. And what do consumers ask in return for this? Feedback on what companies do with their input.

In summary, the new normal in marketing and research is twofold:

* value streams should go *through* consumers, not only *to* them
* every activation initiative companies implement should be the start of a conversation. Companies need to re-verse the equation and start to struc-turally collaborate with consumers.

25

Crowdsourcing, co-creation & structural collaboration: what is **all the buzz** about?

by Tom De Ruyck

In order to define the state of crowd-sourcing, co-creation and structural collaboration with consumers, we talked with 6 leading experts in the field: **Richard Millington** (Managing Director at **Feverbee** and author of *Buzzing Communities*), **Doug Williams** (previously the Co-creation and Open Innovation Expert at **Forrester**, now Principal Analyst at **Innovation Excellence**), **Charles Leadbeater** (author of the bestselling book *We Think*), **Steven Van Belleghem** (former Partner at **InSites Consulting**, author of 2 best-sellers: *The Conversation Manager* & *The Conversation Company* and now Inspirator at **B-Conversational**), **Jeremiah Owyang** (Principal Analyst at **Altimeter Group** and the initiator of *Community Manager Appreciation Day*) & **Yannig Roth** (Research Fellow at crowdsourcing expert **eYeka**).

Richard Millington

Doug Williams

Charles Leadbeater

Steven Van Belleghem

Jeremiah Owyang

Yannig Roth

From trending to mainstream

In the previous article, we touched upon the fact that people are more *social* than ever before. They share their thoughts, feelings, experiences and ideas almost instantly. Consumers are also open to start a true dialogue with brands and the companies behind them.[4] This trend has grown over the last decade and is going mainstream now.[5] Moreover, the experts interviewed agreed that crowdsourcing, co-creation and structural collaboration with consumers are gaining ground as practices in the business world as well. They all notice a general acceptance of these principles and see the pool of true believers and companies that start implementing it within their organizations growing by the day, as *'there are too many opportunities in it, to just ignore the trend'* (dixit Doug Williams).

To get a grip on the trend, it is crucial to define the different ways in which brands can connect and work together with consumers; and to understand how they differ:

Crowdsourcing

Howe describes in his book *Crowdsourcing* how companies outsource tasks to consumers that normally professionals would do.[6] Leadbeater refers to the consumer as a *prosumer* in his book We Think.[7] The main characteristic of crowdsourcing is that it is an open call to the world to help to solve a problem. And everyone may participate. Crowdsourcing can be done as a one-off initiative focused on a specific issue: a challenge that is put online by a company. The crowd is asked to for example send in their ideas for a new campaign or product. **Lay's** *Create Your Taste* campaign is an example of crowdsourcing new product ideas.

A company can also ask consumers to bring in ideas for improvements or new products/services in a more structural way: ongoing and about a wide range of topics. A great example is 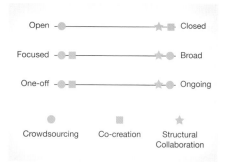 *My Starbucks Idea*,[8] an open online platform launched back in 2008 by **Starbucks** to continuously be able to grasp the ideas from the crowd around its product portfolio and shops. It allows people to post an idea, to vote on ideas from others and to even make those ideas better through conversations with other participants. Both Yannig Roth and Steven Van Belleghem indicate that in most cases, companies use this technique in a too opportunistic way: as a part of a contemporary marketing campaign to just gain reach or as an easy way to get a lot of inspiration for (new) product development.

Co-creation

Co-creation typically takes place having a smaller group of well-chosen people with a rather specific profile. In this case, the goal is to go in-depth on a certain matter and to gain a rich understanding of the issue by being connected with the participants in an intense way, in most cases over a slightly longer period

DNA of Collaboration Methods

of time. Furthermore, the objective is to formulate answers to the relevant business frictions, by working together as a group. An example: we connected the marketing team at **Ben & Jerry's** with extreme brand fans to craft a powerful brand ambassador strategy in 4 weeks' time. This project will be elaborated on the next chapter.

Structural collaboration

In only a minority of the cases the practice of collaboration with consumers is truly embedded within the long-term strategy and the day-to-day business practices of a company. In the end, the important thing is not to just add collaboration to your portfolio of things you do as a company. It is about totally rethinking your way of operating and being committed to listen to the voice of the consumer and make use of the input; every single day and by everyone in the company. Then, you structurally collaborate with the consumer world. Not doing this is a missed opportunity: several studies have shown that companies who do so, typically outperform competitors. As they have consumer input at their fingertips all the time, they are capable of making more informed and more consumer relevant decisions faster.[9] We will go in-depth on what structural collaboration means and how to implement it within an organization in chapter 2.

Each of these three ways of involving the consumer in the business of a company,

....

'Not structurally and deeply collaborating with your key consumers to gain insights in your target group; to improve products, campaigns and brand experiences constantly; is definitely a missed opportunity for most companies'

Steven Van Belleghem

....

are in use today and they will be in use tomorrow. They each have their specific role to play when it comes to connecting companies with their target group. But structural collaboration is the only one in which consumers become day-to-day consultants to the business. It has the power to transform the way business is done.

What to expect?

Charles Leadbeater states that companies should create a bird's nest in which consumers can leave their egg, aka. their feedback and ideas. Today, online communities are the perfect facilitator for these kinds of initiatives. They open up a whole new world of possibilities, both for companies and for consumers. Consumers now get the chance to raise their voice and, above all, get really heard by brands for the first time. Companies on the other hand get a tool to grasp all that feedback and all those ideas in an efficient way. Our own *Social Media Around the World* study highlights that people prefer to work together with brands in smaller, on invitation-only groups.[10] In that case, the chances are higher that they will be listened to and that something will happen with their input.

An often heard argument against collaboration with consumers is that they are not capable of telling you exactly what they really want. **Henry Ford** is probably the most quoted person here: *'If I had asked people what they wanted, they would have asked me for a faster horse'*. Ford was partly right. Consumers will indeed not create a finished product for a company. But they can serve as a vital source of inspiration for the company's experts. It is important to have and set the right expectations here. And, above all, to have the right tools and skills to start the dialogue with the consumer world.

Getting started

The consensus among the interviewees is that there is not one company that does everything right in terms of struc-

....

'All companies should start working together with consumers. The ones that tried it, stopped and now disbelieve, probably just did it the wrong way'

Doug Williams

....

tural collaboration. A lot of companies have made a start. In most cases those initiatives are driven by visionary CxOs or intrapreneurs with a strong belief in the power of listening to the consumer. There is a common belief that there already is a wide range of best practices out there and that companies do not need to reinvent the wheel. They need to in-source the expertise and bright people within the company need to be the driving force behind embedding the practice into the daily business.

4 stages to make a start with structural collaboration can be identified:

1. **Defining the objectives:** it is crucial to define the objectives properly from the start. Clear objectives include agreeing on KPIS that need to be measured and standards that need to be reached. Without the latter, it is impossible to prove what the initiative adds to the business. It is important to match the objectives with the current company culture and business practices and to move forward step by step. Change does not just happen, it needs to be managed.

2. **Securing the necessary resources:** it is crucial to have the support from higher management to make a jump start and to get the necessary budgets and organizational alignment from the start. In some companies a successful pilot will need to be done before structural resources can be claimed.

....

'Companies must have their internal teams, resources, processes and programs aligned in order to be successful'

Jeremiah Owyang

....

3. **Creating & managing the community:** Richard Millington is very clear on this one: *'There is a big difference between enabling consumers to collaborate with you and motivating them to do it'*. Companies are typically very good at the former and terrible at the latter. The biggest mistake companies make is offering huge rewards; this lowers motivation in the long term. What consumers want is simply to have greater self-efficacy. The idea that they are having an impact on the world. Recognizing people for the great contributions they make is what counts. Moreover, people from different backgrounds or cultures will have different expectations, which implies that managing a community never follows a *one size fits all formula*.

4. **Adding value to the business:** in the end it is all about return on investment. Getting great input is one thing, making sure it is used within the company is another. In order to get everybody on board, the ambassadors of the initiative should not only measure its success, they should also share and celebrate it within the organization. That will keep the (r)evolution going.

The future

What will the future bring? Jeremiah Owyang envisions a different future for the companies that have and have not gained this new capability: *'Consumers want to be connected with companies and they have a plethora of ideas to improve products and services. Companies can source their energy to improve. The brands that harness this have the opportunity to thrive'.*

Structurally collaborating with consumers has the potential to become the new norm. But companies need to be careful. They cannot take the consumers' willingness to participate in companies' initiatives for granted. Most communities do not give members a true sense of having impact. They let members give their opinions but then fail to act upon it. They make the community feel powerless. When a company develops a community, it gives the community a sense of power over the organization. The community becomes an external *Board of Advisors*. It is key to not take this lightly. It is up to us all, to make sure that we can keep the true spirit of collaboration alive, also at the consumers' side.

TWEETAWAYS

Marketing is evolving from a
dominantly 'to consumers' approach to
a 'through consumers' approach.
@Niels_InSites

Companies should start working together with consumers: those that tried,
stopped and now disbelieve, probably
just did it the wrong way.
@DougWilliamsMHD

Companies can source their energy
from consumers to improve: brands that
harness this have the opportunity to
thrive.
@jowyang

The difference between crowdsourcing & structural collaboration is what
distinguishes a one-night stand from a
relationship: commitment.
@tomderuyck

Companies should create a bird's nest
in which consumers can leave their egg,
aka their feedback and ideas.
@LeadbeaterCh

2

From
co-creation
to structural
collaboration

Bringing consumers into the business, all the way up to **the boardroom**

by Tom De Ruyck & Niels Schillewaert

Becoming an open and agile company today, in order to win tomorrow

Most of you will probably agree: the past 5 years have been absolutely crazy for those who are running a business. Radical changes took place, at a speed never seen before, leading to a new reality both in the world of the consumer and in the context in which business is done.

Through social media, consumers have gained the power to make or break brands. Over the last years, hundreds of case studies were written on how consumers can praise a brand and help out to spread a message or improve a product. But we know as many cases where ordinary consumers bring brands down in only a matter of nanoseconds, as is stated by **Unilever**'s CEO **Paul Polman**. The lesson here is, as a company, you no longer have full control of what is being said about and done with your brands. Like it or not, consumers will talk about brands and the products and services they offer, both in good and in bad times. Moreover, consumers do not only want to talk about brands, they also want to talk with the company and the people behind it. Our ▢ *Social Media around the World* study states that more than 4 out of 5 consumers

want to collaborate with companies they like, about topics they have an affinity with.[1] They prefer to do this in an intimate online environment which offers real interaction with the brand and allows them to really influence the decision-making. Nowadays, companies have to deal with truly empowered consumers. This is even more the case for Generation Y:[2] they were born in the digital age and raised by their parents in such a way that they feel they can really make their own choices. Companies need to listen better to what the empowered consumer has to say and take advantage of it to improve their performance.

From a business perspective, companies globally are now confronted with a hard economic climate. But despite this new situation, expectations from consumers keep on rising and the competitive landscape keeps on changing, at an even higher speed than before. In this climate of harder, better and faster, companies need to make themselves stronger every day in order to outperform the competition and win.

From co-creation to structural collaboration

In this new world, it seems to be vital for companies to embrace the empowered consumer and to be able to react quickly to what happens both in the consumer world and in the daily business reality. In other words, it is crucial to become an open and agile company today, in order to be one of the winners tomorrow. Only a minority of companies have already reached this stage. Most companies are still stuck in one-way communication with their customers. Moreover, they jump from one campaign or project to the next. There is no continuous interaction or dialogue with the customer. This means that they miss out on opportunities that are popping up in-between two marketing campaigns or ad-hoc research projects. The new norm we are living in, demands that companies start a continuous dialogue with the consumer. To listen constantly, to work together on projects and to react quickly to what happens in the

world around them. The latter asks for an agile organization: one that can move really fast. However, this is extremely difficult if you are organized in silos, as most companies still are. The reality is that departments pass projects on to one another. They do not work together on projects simultaneously. This does not benefit the overall outcome of those projects nor the speed at which they are executed. Think of how long it takes to bring a new product to the market. It literally takes years before it makes it from the R&D labs where it was created to the marketing team that works on the launch strategy.

It is important to start working today on becoming an open and agile company. It is the biggest opportunity ever to outperform the competition, by being one of the first to gain these new strategic capabilities.

Consumers to the rescue

In order to become an open company, you need to start the dialogue with all your stakeholders, especially with your consumers. They are probably the best consultants you could hire. Consumers have a lot of knowledge about a brand's history. Knowing that most marketers in FMCG companies change jobs every 2 years, those consumers probably survived several generations of (brand) managers. People who have an affinity with your brand also show an extraordinary engagement: they want their brand to perform well. In a community we ran for the ice cream brand **Ben & Jerry's** - in which we worked with highly engaged brand fans - it was striking to see how extremely critical they were towards what the brand managers did.[3] And in the end, customers are always right. They are the ones who buy the company's products and services and who ensure that the company has a business.

To make optimal use of their consulting power, a company needs to start a two-way dialogue with consumers, rather than to just listen to what consumers have to say about their products, services or brands on social media, as the latter does not give them the chance to work together with consumers on very specific questions. In order to get the maximum out of this dialogue, it is best to bring a larger group of consumers together on a closed online community platform over a longer period of time: a *Market Research Online Community (MROC)*.[4] What is the difference between this way of listening to and working with consumers and the more traditional way of interviews or focus groups? The similarities and differences lie in its main characteristics:

- **Closed or on invitation only:** just like in traditional qualitative research, a company's secrets are safe. Other than on open crowdsourcing platforms, the facilitator decides who has access to the online community platform and has full control over the profile of the people who are taken on board. Moreover, a confidentiality agreement between the participant and the company can be settled. Nothing different from traditional techniques so far.

- **Online community platform:** first of all, online means convenience for all parties involved. Nobody needs to travel to take part in or to follow the research. This leads to

39

a lower cost per participant on the one hand and a more convenient way to follow the discussion and be immersed in the consumer world for business people on the other hand. Secondly, a greater geographical coverage is possible. You can bring people from one side of a country together with those from the other side. Or even work across different countries. Thirdly, the online community platform itself allows to deploy a multitude of different research techniques: individual tasks, 1-on-1 interaction with participants or interactive group discussions and brainstorms. On the platform one can perform observational (blog research), qualitative (interviews, focus groups and bulletin board discussions) and basic quantitative research (a variety of multi-media tools and short digital surveys) via the multitude of next-generation online research tools that are available. Although mainly being a qualitative research tool, we may speak of a *fusion* research platform, given the richness of research possibilities. A final advantage of a community: it gives participants a place to provide the company with unsolicited feedback. Every platform has a corner where members can talk about what they want. In most cases they use this place to raise issues

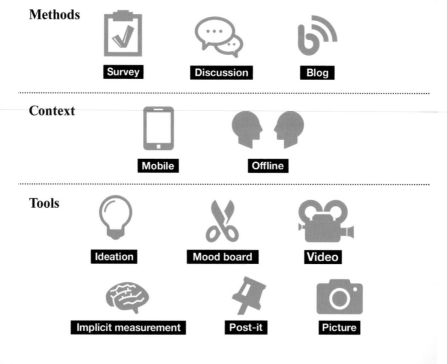

Research techniques to enrich the online community experience

that were not yet discussed within the research topics started by the moderator, but that they find relevant for the sponsoring brand. One could see this space in the community as a bird's nest where participants can leave their very own thoughts, feedback and ideas.

- **Larger group of participants:** we most often work with 50 to 150 members in our communities. The advantage of working with a larger group of people is that you can include a wide diversity of profiles, bringing in more and different opinions. Members also build on each other's idea, which leads to cross-fertilization. All of this brings more and richer insights to the table. Working with a limited number of people still makes it possible to ask probing questions as a community moderator and to have an in-depth qualitative discussion with and among the members.

- **Longer period of time (asynchronous engagement):** working together with your consumers for several weeks or months or even structurally on a day-to-day basis helps you to get to know your target group like never before and to tackle a wide range of issues at the same time. Time gives members the chance to think, rethink and fine-tune their opinions throughout, leading to more elaborated and mature answers. Having more time also allows

companies to work together with customers from generating the initial insight/idea until the preparation of the product or campaign launch. This development can happen on an as-we-go basis: iterative and hands-on reworking of concepts or stimulus materials. Structural collaboration means that you always have customers at your side when you need to make important decisions. Within 24 hours you will have answers to urgent questions. However the latter is only possible if your community is always on.

The table on the next page gives an overview of online consumer listening and interaction methods. It compares research communities with other asynchronous - not real time - methods on the dimensions discussed above. Having a research community to work closely with makes you more open as a company. But it will take more to become agile as well; you need to structurally collaborate with your community of consumers: almost every single day, for most business issues and across all departments dealing with the consumer. That is why we prefer using the term Consumer Consulting Board rather than Market Research Online Community, as it gives a better summary of what it is or should become. The name is the best indication of the place that such a research community deserves within an organization. It is not just next-generation market research technology. It is not about the technology at all, which is

	Blogs	Bulletin Boards	Online Research Communities	Community Panels	Access Panels
Description	1 on 1 asynchronous discussions and observations	Asynchronous focus groups or short term discussions with small samples	Asynchronous discussions with medium-sized samples and variable duration	Internet access panels with interactive social media applications	Internet access panels
Duration	Short	Short	Short - Long Term	Long Term	Long Term
Intensity	High	High	High - Medium	Low	None
Direction	Bidirectional	Bidirectional	Bidirectional	More unidirectional - some interactional	Unidirectional
Research techniques	Qualitative only	Qualitative only	Qualitative only	Quantitative, some qualitative	Quantitative

Overview of online consumer listening and interaction methods

no more than a facilitator. What counts is that the company actively listens to its customers. And that the input of this *Board of advisors* is used every day to steer the daily operations and to make better-informed decisions much faster. Only then we can truly speak of structural collaboration with the consumer.

H.J. Heinz Netherlands has been using a Consumer Consulting Board for over 4 years now. It is a community of 150 females responsible for purchases, all into food and cooking for their families. The different brand teams at H.J. Heinz are all making use of the Board, as are the people at customer service and R&D. The platform is managed and moderated by us as an agency, jointly with the *Consumer Insights department*. Another illustration of structural collaboration is what we do together with the advertis-

ing agency **Famous**. Their Consumer Consulting Board is helping them to make more impactful advertisements for their clients by being connected with real consumers in all stages of the creative process: getting the initial insights, gaining feedback on first ideas of the creative team and moving towards a final end deliverable in iterative loops, fueled with consumer feedback. ⬚ A final example is the global community we ran for **Heineken** with young club-goers in the 20 hottest cities on the planet. Together with these youngsters, emerging designers from major design capitals, the different teams at Heineken (design, marketing, communications and PR) and an external PR agency, we co-created a vision of the club of tomorrow over somewhat more than a year.[5] From observing their nightlife experiences to getting feedback on sketches and concepts up to the actual building of the club in Milan during the annual design fair, consumer input and feedback was used at all times and by all parties involved. It is a great example of the second meaning of structural collaboration: different stakeholders working together around the consumer community, with only one thing on the agenda: being successful in the market by working on what the consumer needs or expects.

H.J. Heinz Food community

Heineken Concept Club community

Adapt your Consumer Consulting Board to your company's DNA

Structural collaboration does not happen overnight.[6] It asks for change management within the company: budgets need to be (re)allocated, clear objectives need to be defined and key people internally need to be convinced of the use of the community and the concept of structural collaboration. Some companies can make a jumpstart; in other companies it will take a successful pilot project to get everybody on board. In that case, it is a matter of thinking big with the end goal in mind, but starting small with a pilot project.

One of the misunderstandings about the use of Consumer Consulting Boards is that they solely serve the innovation needs of companies. Nothing is less true as they are used equally often to generate insights, develop new products or services, fine-tune brand strategies, co-create advertising campaigns and improve customer experiences. The approach is also suitable for every kind of industry. Although there is a need for slight adaptations in the method used, the community approach is successfully applied to business-to-business environments and to the world of patients and health care professionals.

43

Get close to your customer

Uncover new insights

Business Objectives

Drive consumer experience & action

Generate & craft ideas and concepts

Business objectives of Consumer Consulting Boards

It is vital that you adapt the use of the Consumer Consulting Board to the current company culture and practices. The more it matches with current business planning, the better. **Cloetta**, a European chocolates and sweets manufacturer, aligns the use of its Consumer Consulting Board with its marketing plans. Input from the consumer world is asked before key decision-making moments during the year. From an organizational point of view, it can be useful to opt for a staged roll-out: including objective by objective, brand by brand or department by department. That way you can change the way things are done step by step and plan them. The most important thing is to always keep the end goal of structural collaboration in mind and aim for it.

Making consumers wanting to be a part of your Board

What does it take to establish and manage a successful Consumer Consulting Board? In this paragraph we will share our recipe with you. These best practices are based on more than 7 years of fundamental research within our ForwaR&D Lab (in collaboration with different academic institutions), a wide range of experiments and the experience of running over 300 communities for our clients.

From our research-on-research, we know that the high performers in a community - the ones who participate frequently and share the most interesting insights and ideas - are the ones who show brand and/or topic identification 📱. They are a fan of the brand behind the community and/or they are more interested in the discussed topic(s) than the average person. This makes that we work with people who are not only *interested* in what we are going to do, but who are also *interesting* to listen to. They are the ones who will stimulate our thinking and push things forward.

Through our research, we learned that we need at least 30 answers to a given question in order to make a descent qualitative analysis. We noticed a saturation effect around the 30th answer:

people tend to tell us more of the same thing from that point onwards.[7] A natural form of lurking pops-up. People read through the input of others and feel that they have nothing else to contribute anymore. In a short-term community of for example 3 weeks, people participate very intensely. They know that there is a start and an end date; they fit it in within their lives. Therefore we need less people to reach the required 30 answers. In communities with a longer duration, we notice that people tend to participate in waves. They are more active during certain periods than during others. We compensate for that by adding more members to those communities. A 3-week community requires at least 50 intensively participating members. Communities of 3 months and longer on the other hand ask for 150 participants for achieving our goal (or more if one works with different subgroups within the community). Adding more people than required would not result in any additional insights. We would simply start generating conversations simply for the sake of the conversation. Another reason why 150 is more or less the upper limit for the (sub-)group sizes we work with: beyond this point, it becomes difficult for the participants to interact with each other and for the moderator to ask follow-up questions.

Having the right number of participants with the right profile on a great multimedia social platform is not enough. True participant engagement is required in order to be successful. To boost the level of engagement, the community members are briefed during a half-hour session in which the moderator explains to them what the community is all about, what the brand is behind it all and what the overall goal of the project is. The main aspects of the topics on the agenda are shared and feedback on it is asked: *'Is there anything else that you as a customer want to talk about with us?'* Furthermore, they get a clear overview of what is in it for them: a small financial incentive, weekly feedback on the progress of the project and, from time to time, a surprise from the sponsoring brand. Our research in collaboration with the **University of Maastricht** has shown that organizing these kick-off sessions boosts engagement and activity on the community from the very start.

In order to keep participants engaged over time it is important to pre-define and strategize the number, types and order of questions that will be asked to the members in a conversation guide. It is important that there is a storyline. Participants need to get the feeling that they are working on something bigger and that they are almost part of the company behind the community. Another crucial element is building in enough variation when it comes to the tasks to perform. It is important to have a balance between harder-to-answer questions or time-consuming tasks and fun topics or more straightforward questions. The portfolio of different research methodologies available needs to be used in order to make it an interesting

45

and surprising journey for the members of the Board.

Another way of turning it into an engaging experience for the participants is to add gamification elements to the community: applying the principles and psychology behind games to motivate people and enhance their performance.[8] This can be done on 4 different levels:[9]

- **Question level:** turning ordinary questions into small challenges ensures that participants spend more time on answering them. An example is what we did in *Crushed Ice*, a global community project for **MTV Networks** with 100 cool GenYers in the 10 hottest cities on earth. When searching for the hotspots in their city, the specific question was turned into a challenge: *'Can you come up with as many hotspots in your city as possible? Based on all proof that is posted, the MTV jury will decide which city officially deserves the title of Hottest City on the Planet.'* The difference in the level of enthusiasm about normal questions and this type of challenges is significant.

- **Individual level:** to reward members for great achievements in the community, they receive badges which give them a certain status. The badges indicate that they were part of a specific project or that they significantly contributed to an important breakthrough. The badges appear on the profile page of the community members. One could compare it with how the army honors soldiers for their bravery and persistence.

- **Group level:** the beauty of working with a diverse group of people is that it leads to rich discussions. In order to stimulate interaction, which always leads to a better outcome, one can organize battles of arguments between groups with different opinions or ask groups of people with the same interest to play against another team. An illustration of the latter comes from a community project we conducted together with the team at **Unilever Global R&D**: *Consumer&U* [10]. In this 100-participants community we created 3 sub-groups which could each ideate around a different product category. In order to let them think harder, we organized a game. The group which came up with the highest quality input by the end of the week got access to a secret room in the community. We noticed that the activity level in the community went up and that members within each group were stimulating each other to aim higher. The winning team got the keys to the secret room in which the latest *Magnum ice cream innovation* was showcased. And of course there were a couple of questions about it. In the end, it is all about making your agenda of topics a surprising and engaging experience for the members.

- **Community level:** a last option is to build milestones that the members should try and reach by a given date. If the target is reached, a special prize or gift is unlocked. In the global community for Heineken to envision the *Club of Tomorrow*, we gave the participants a target of 2,000 comments by the end of the second week; if they succeeded, they would get to see some first ideas and sketches from the designers.[11] This is something one should do anyway, but by making it a part of something bigger, it stimulates curiosity and pushes people to higher performance levels.

Examples of rewarding badges

By comparing the meta-data of gamified and non-gamified communities, we learned that if you gamify your community on the 4 levels described above, it will lead to 7 times more on-topic arguments.[12] This means that you do not get more answers, but richer answers. People just think harder for you by spending more time while answering the questions and performing the tasks.

Thinking different, anywhere and anytime

Qualitative research is also about letting people think more emotionally, creatively and contextually. That is why one also needs to use a series of projective or creative techniques. Some of them are online translations of traditional techniques; others are totally new, inspired by the new possibilities available in the online world. An illustration of the variety of options available online is what we did with **Chiquita** in a project in which they wanted to discover the mental and physical benefits of eating (and drinking) fruit (juices). The outcomes of the project were used as ammunition for the launch campaign of their smoothie offering. We started a 3-week community with 50 participants. Half of them were living healthily and already eating a lot of fruit; the other half was living unhealthy,

47

eating almost no fruit at all. In the first week of the community, we explored the topic and held a discussion about what a healthy lifestyle is and what the role of eating/drinking fruit (juices) is. We were following a more or less typical discussion guide of a traditional focus group. In the second week, participants were invited to become part of a scientific experiment. They were asked to swap lives. The ones who were already eating enough fruit were kindly asked to stop doing so. The unhealthy group on the other hand received a basket full of fresh fruit and smoothies, delivered at their door 3 times in that same week. Over the course of 7 days, all participants kept a diary and received short daily surveys on their mental and physical energy levels. All of this entailed a rich understanding into what it is like to change behavior. This resulted in powerful insights into the mental and physical benefits of eating/drinking fruit (juices). In order to understand which of these insights were most relevant to consumers and to identify the most important aspects to schedule in the launch campaign, we organized a battle of arguments between the 2 groups. They needed to convince one another to change lifestyles, based on the list of mental and physical benefits generated during the first 2 weeks of the community. This project is a perfect illustration of a community as a true fusion research platform, which allows to conduct research activities that were simply impossible before via more traditional research methods.

In order to capture emotions and experiences in the heat of the moment, communities need to be accessible via mobile devices as well. Our meta-research shows that mobile access boosts the engagement of participants. Moreover, it unlocks a new kind of input. Through the mobile device, members provide us with more personal and contextual information: stories illustrated with photos or videos, next to in-the-moment reactions and feedback. During a project for ⬚ **Campbell's** in Australia on the evolution of the food culture in the country, we could almost see and follow in real-time how people went shopping for ingredients, how they prepared their meals and with whom they were having those meals.[13]

Our mobile app: example of the Campbell's Come Dine with Me community

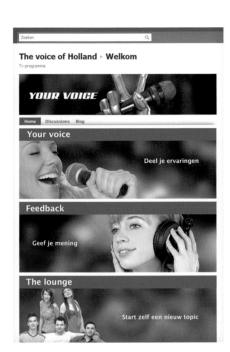

Facebook integration: example of The Voice of Holland community

Today, due to changes in consumer behavior, researchers are more than ever forced to do the research where the consumer is: online, through mobile devices and on social platforms. An illustration of this trend is our Consumer Consulting Board for the television format *The Voice*. We had to evaluate the different aspects of the show, the product placement within and the advertisement around it, while the show was being broadcast. It would have been difficult to get people into a traditional type of research here. We noticed that during the show a lot of chatting was going on among viewers on the *The Voice Facebook page*. So, in order to realize our goal, we integrated our community platform into the Facebook fan page. That way we were able to do the research in the consumers' natural habitat and in the heat of the moment.

When the board members take over

By selecting the right number of members, with the right profile, getting and keeping them engaged, letting them think harder and differently, everywhere and anytime, we collected a huge amount of rich and meaningful data. In order to get the most out of this, we need to walk our own talk. Our advice to companies is to work together with consumers to do a better job. Researchers need to do exactly the same and invite members to become part of the research process by becoming co-researchers.[14] They can help us with moderation, analysis/interpretation and reporting. For co-moderation (participants become the co-pilots of the professional moderator), meta-research indicates that it stimulates the interaction between members and the richness of the discussion: twice as much interaction and 25% of additional on-topic arguments. Asking help to a sub-set of the community to analyze specific posts that the professional researcher does not fully understand brings between 20% and 40% of additional insights to the table, depending on the subject. A great illustration of the power of co-analysis or crowd-interpretation lies in an international project for Heinz to gain insights about ketchup usage, where ordinary consumers did a better job in analyzing pictures and stories of others than the marketers in the European HQ.

The use of co-researchers in the Campbell's Come Dine with Me community, the H.J. Heinz Food Community and the Philips Sleepwell community

Finally, while writing your report, it is important that you get your final conclusions absolutely right. That is why it can be beneficial to organize a dry-run of your main conclusions to a sub-set of your Consumer Consulting Board. In a study we did for ☐ **Philips** about sleeping problems among business people in China, we knew we had 2 specific issues to tackle: when doing research in China talking about a medical condition is rather sensitive and due to the culture there is quite some socially desirable answering patterns. We invited 10 additional members who we asked to not participate in the community, but to only observe it. We presented our main findings to this group of people and asked them to comment on our conclusions. In this case, 14% of our final conclusions were challenged or nuanced by the co-researchers in our community. In the end, these particular adjustments turned out to be crucial to position Philips' products correctly in the Chinese market. It is clear what co-researchers bring to the table: they fill a researcher's blind spots. Researchers cannot possibly know and fully understand every single target group or context, simply because they are not living all those different lives. Involving co-researchers is not about participants taking the job of the professional moderator, researcher or consultant. It is about inviting participants on board to help you do an even better job. Let's walk our own talk and work together with the crowd.

The path
towards structural
collaboration

In the previous paragraphs the reasons behind establishing a Consumer Consulting Board were outlined and details on how to set it up and run the community on a daily basis were discussed. The final part of this article deals with the question of how to make the community a real success and let it be of true value for the company. Here are some key success factors that we came across while interviewing (senior) executives from global brands who have a Consumer Consulting Board (amongst others H.J. Heinz, Unilever, Microsoft and Danone):[15]

C-level involvement

Support is not enough. Senior executives need to be involved and to lead by example. Important decisions are not made without involving the members of the Consumer Consulting Board.

Create buy-in & discover your knowledge gaps

Before starting, it is important to get everyone on board and to create an understanding of the concept of a Consumer Consulting Board. Furthermore, it is good to create an inventory of the knowledge available in

the company about the subjects to work on. There are several ways of making this an engaging experience for the stakeholders involved. At **Air France and KLM** for example we did this by playing a board game with the internal stakeholders during the kick-off workshop.[16]

Measuring KPIs and celebrating successes

In order to demonstrate the return on investment it is important to define KPIs upfront, based on the objectives, to measure them smartly and to celebrate and share success stories. KPIs can be a mix of aspects linked to one or more of the following categories: acquiring fresh and fast knowledge to make better decisions, creating a consumer-centric-thinking company culture and showing the world that the company is listening to and collaborating with its consumers.

Impactful communication of results both internally and towards the external world

- **Internal leverage:** in order to make sure something is done with the research results and to build a consumer-centric thinking culture within companies, we need to use a 3-step approach to communicate to the business: engage, inspire and activate.[17] By doing this, researchers think more like marketers. Marketers try to create as many of the right touchpoints as possible between their brand(ed message) and the consumer world. In research communication it is beneficial to create different contact moments between the voice of the consumer and the stakeholders in the business. It immerses them into the world of the consumer and positively affects their hearts, minds and actions.

▶ **Engage** is about confronting the research users with the consumer world and with their own (lack of) knowledge about the matter. We try to create positive disruption: making them feel a little bit uncomfortable about their current view on the subject and curious about the final outcome while the project is still running. This can be done by organizing quizzes about the first outcomes or by distributing offline posters with striking quotes within the company's premises.

▶ In the **Inspire** phase we inspire the internal stakeholders with the gained insights in an interactive workshop. Sometimes the audience is too big to give a presentation to. This was the case in the Unilever R&D project where we needed to report back to a group of more than 500 people. In order to do this, we created a consumer news website on which two articles about the consumer world were shared every day, during the whole duration of the community.[18] Another obstacle can be reporting

Interactive infographic of the Heineken Concept Club community

to very creative audiences, such as in our *Heineken The Club project*. To be impactful among this audience we turned over 3,000 consumer stories and pictures into 30 compact insights, ⃞ in an interactive infographic which guided the designers through a young club-goers' night out.[19]

▶ Finally, the research outcome needs to be used effectively. In the **Activate** stage of a workshop we work with the results and turn insights into actions through ideation, concept-writing exercises and the like. In order to make sure that a project has an after-life we create deliverables that encourage to be used afterwards. An example are the city guides we created for the senior executives of MTV Networks based on the tips for hotspots we received from GenY'ers around the world. It allowed the MTV executives to immerse themselves into the world of their target group when being on a business trip.[20]

▶ Using this approach of communicating findings makes the results really well-used. Moreover, it makes that employees develop a kind of consumer feeling next to their gut feeling, by being immersed into the consumer world.

● **External leverage:** listening to the outside world as a company is something consumers expect nowadays. Grasp this opportunity and communicate about the fact that you do it. One can unlock this untapped communication potential by communicating about:

  ▶ **Process:** communicate to the world that you have a Consumer Consulting Board. One of the ways to do that is as did the CEO of **Telenet**, a Belgian Telco company. He made an open request to the world: *'Who wants to be part of our board and help us improve our products?'*

  ▶ **Outcomes:** showcase the end results of your collaboration with consumers. Heineken launched the club they co-created during the *Annual Design Fair* in Milan.

  ▶ **Findings:** share interesting findings with the world or use them to tell your story as a brand (together with the members of your community). Chiquita used the findings of our fruit and smoothie study in their advertisement to convince consumers to change behavior.

53

How we engaged, inspired and activated Air France and KLM, Unilever R&D and MTV Networks

What it brings to the table

What does structural collaboration with consumers bring to companies who do it well and who communicate about it in the best possible way, both internally and towards the external world? We see that companies that work together with consumers come up with more consumer-relevant products/services and marketing actions. This was proven in a project for H.J. Heinz in which ideas generated by consumers in a community and ideas generated by marketers were battling with one another in a concept screener. Ideas generated by marketers were significantly more perceived as being unique. Ideas originating through the community on the other hand were evaluated as more consumer relevant and obtained a higher buying intention in the same test among a representative sample of the population. In a different study in collaboration with the **University of Wageningen**, we compared two different pack designs for the same product. A claim was added to one of the packs: *'co-created with consumers'*. The other pack did not carry any such claim. Again, it was found that the pack with the claim was perceived as more consumer-relevant and had a higher buying intention.

This shows that it is not only about performing the co-creation exercise; it is also about communicating wisely about the fact that you do it. It will lead to a humanization of your company and brand. Companies that are open to the outside world actually do something consumers expect from companies nowadays. They are perceived as more contemporary and genuine. And through the positive (brand) experience you give the members, you create positive conversations about your brand and mostly also brand advocates for life.

Last but not least, by having the consumers' input at your fingertips 24/7, you gain the ability to move rapidly. It also makes that departments work on a project together. And it is the consumer who determines the agenda, rather than the hidden agenda of departments within the company. It means that, internally, things move quicker as well. The end result is that you become a more agile company. And that type of company will be tomorrow's winners.

Make it an evolution instead of a revolution

The way to becoming a truly open and agile company is a journey that asks for a step-by-step approach. Some companies will immediately make a start with structural collaboration.

THE perfect storm IS HERE

Others start a pilot project before moving forward. Some companies start by using it for a specific product category or brand or within a specific department of the company and extend it to other categories and brands over time, thus intensifying the frequency and intensity at which the Consumer Consulting Board is used within different parts of the business. No matter how you start, it will always be an evolution rather than a revolution. Change never happens overnight.

The main thing is that you move towards the end goal of structural collaboration. It is about aiming for the moment that for most business objectives, almost every single day and across all departments, the input from the Consumer Consulting Board is used to make better-informed decisions faster than ever before. And when that goal is reached,

it's time for the final stage: having an ambassador of the voice of the consumer in the boardroom of the company (*the CCO, Chief Consumer Officer*).

Let's start today. The perfect storm is here: consumers are ready for it; they are even waiting for us. The technology to facilitate the ongoing dialogue with your Board is there as well. And the recipe to make it all happen has been fine-tuned, based on years of experience.

Good luck on your journey towards becoming a truly consumer-centric-thinking company!

In the second part of this chapter we examine how all the different stakeholders (our internal community team, our researchers, our moderators, the community participants & our clients, ...) experience a Consumer Consulting Board.

Alexandra Ardean

Wim De Wever

Oana Frentiu

Content Manager

Research Consultant

Moderator

Planning & Network Management

The content manager holds the final accountability for any project. He/she understands the client('s needs) proposes and elaborates the best research approach for answering the research questions.

The research consultant is mainly responsible for managing the project from a research perspective. He/she is omnipresent during the entire project: from composing a conversation guide to the analysis and reporting afterwards.

The moderator is in charge of the actual moderation. In the case of an international project, our research consultants work together with a team of local moderators out of our *Global Community Moderator Network*. Our local moderators are briefed by the planner and the research consultant.

The planner is responsible for working out a detailed project planning based upon the project needs and the required and available resources. The outcome serves as an essential framework for all project stakeholders.

The making of...
...through the eyes of a PM²

Project & Method Manager

The project & method manager (PM²) is the internal account manager: the liaison between the content manager, research consultant and moderator on the one hand and the entire project implementation team on the other hand. He/she is accountable for the full implementation and the community member recruitment process within each individual community project. The role of the PM² is not limited to coordinating the execution of client projects; it also includes working on the continuous improvement of our operational quality and optimizing our processes. InSites Consulting has 3 PM²'s who coordinate all community projects from a practical perspective: Wim, Oana and Alexandra.

On the following pages you can follow how a community project comes to life, featuring the following project team members:

IT Project Manager

Recruiter

Quality Control

Designer

The IT'er takes care of all technical programming and implementations required for a project, including the online recruitment survey and the community platform with the necessary research tools and plug-ins.

The recruiter ensures that we find the right community members, on time, by applying to the most suitable recruitment sources. Recruitment includes the careful screening (or selection) of the community members but also builds the engagement towards the future participants via different communication channels.

We have introduced quite some checks in our implementation processes, by which we are sure to guarantee the highest quality both to our customers and to our participants. The quality controller is involved in all phases of the implementation process to perform the necessary checks and tests.

The designer works out a unique look-and-feel for the community platform, suitable for the specific brand, topic and target group, but also respecting the trusted InSites Consulting design framework. The custom branded community guarantees an optimal user experience for both the participants and the client.

From co-creation to structural collaboration

Research questions?

Briefing the team!

58

1 Client kick-off

Kick-off with the client to discuss the research questions & needs with the content manager and the research consultant, followed by an introduction to the research method.

2 Internal kick-off

The project details, including the target group and the most suitable recruitment approach, are determined during an internal kick-off with the research consultant and the project & method manager (PM²).

3 Internal planning and briefing

PM² and planning draw up a detailed project planning and allocate the necessary capacity in the agendas of the composed project team. The PM² organizes an internal briefing with the project implementation team to inform them about the screening survey and the recruitment approach.

4 Recruitment survey programming

The IT'er programs the screening survey while the recruiter makes the necessary preparations for the community member recruitment. The quality control team takes care of some technical and textual checks before the online survey is launched. The PM² keeps an eye on a smooth implementation flow.

et's create a clear guide...

Creating the online platform....

5 Recruiting community members

The recruiter makes sure he/she finds the right community members and provides regular progress updates to the PM². The future community members are invited to participate in the screening survey via an e-mail. Further engagement is built via a subsequent confirmation e-mail and a moderator call, all of this followed up by the recruiter.

6 Conversation guide creation

Simultaneously with the recruitment, the research consultant takes the lead in working on the detailed research approach, in close consultation with the content manager and the client. All this results in a conversation guide functioning as the *community script*.

7 Briefing of specs and design

The PM² summarizes the wishes from the different stakeholders and briefs our technical and design teams. The designer is informed by the PM² and works out the look-and-feel for the community. After client approval the final design serves as 'input' for the next phase: the implementation of the platform.

8 Platform implementation

Right after the PM² has validated the technical community specifications, the IT'er begins with the technical and design implementation of the community platform, together with the set-up of the kick-off sessions.

Check!

Ready for take-off!

9 Quality checks

The PM² informs the quality control team, which comes in for a second time to do some final checks on the community platform right before we go live!

10 Kick-off with members

Kick-off sessions are planned to allow the moderator to inform the community members about the project roadmap and the participants' role. The PM² makes sure the recruiter sends the necessary log-in instructions towards the community members so they can get access to their respective kick-off session and the actual community right after.

11 Community goes live!

Our enthusiastic community members log in after the kick-off session, start socializing in the welcome thread and start to participate in the first tasks the moderator has posted online.

12 Community moderation

Fresh discussion threads and challenges are initiated by the moderator according to the schedule prepared in the conversation guide. All community members get regular updates on the latest tasks and info via newsletters sent out by the moderator. The moderator can consult the PM² who keeps an eye on the community activity level as well.

Turning conversations into insights

Eureka!

13 Analysis & reporting

During the moderation period, the research consultant (in close contact with the moderator) already does some basic data analysis and has intermediary feedback moments with the client. This feedback might still impact and reshape some future community threads and tasks.

14 Closing of the community

After a cooling down period, the PM² asks the IT'er to *officially* close the community for the members. The recruiter makes sure that the most valuable participants get a reward immediately, along with a closing e-mail message referring to a satisfaction survey.

15 Writing the full story

The research consultant and the content manager are in charge of the final analysis and the reporting of the rich community data, clearly answering all the client's research questions & needs raised at the start.

16 Client workshop

The moment of truth! The final report will be unveiled to the client. The research consultant and content manager will expound the complete community story in person, in an interactive way.

From co-creation to structural collaboration

Inside the Board

Rooms

The different discussion topics are featured in dedicated rooms to focus the mindset of the participant on the type or content of the challenges, ranging from forum discussions and diaries to ideation challenges and short surveys.

Latest topics

As not all participants are joining the discussions daily, topics are posted in clusters and the most recent topics are featured on the home page.

Who's online

Although the discussions on the Consumer Consulting Board are asynchronous, featuring online members enhances to the group feeling.

Consumer **Consulti**

Home | Blog | Forum

Your life   **Your product usage**   **Your feed**

The social corner

Latest topics

Friends	Topics
Your life	**How was your weekend?**
Your ideas	**New Ideas - What Works?**
Your feedback	**The Final Debate**

Who's online?

 Layla_Jones

 Robert_Smith

Board

InSites Consulting

Your ideas

April 18th 2013

April 17th 2013

Number of posts

4316
reactions

Time left until the revelation of the brand new concept you have created together with us.

14	**12**	**00**	**35**
DAYS	HRS	MIN	SEC

Welcome!

Nice to meet you! I'm moderator Marie, and I will guide you through the community and tasks for the next 3 months.

If you have questions, feel free to e-mail me at marie@communitymod.com!

New blog!

Customized skin

The customized design of the platform intensifies the participant idenitification with the topic and/or the brand. The design is used in all touchpoints, from short surveys to newsletters to guarantee a consistent activation.

Activating members

It is surprising how many comments consumers share in a couple of weeks. Featuring the number of reactions on the home page provides an intrinsic motivation to do even better. Of course, milestone numbers - 2500 comments for example - are celebrated!

Countdown

Awareness around special events or deadlines is created by featuring a live countdown on the home page.

New blog posts

To guide the attention of participants to the most important discussions, they can be visually highlighted on the homepage.

63

From co-creation to structural collaboration

Your custom designed Board

Hannes Willaert

Designer

At InSites Consulting, we truly believe in the power of design. That is why we have a team of designers who create custom made skins for all our Consumer Consulting Boards. In consultation with the client, our designers create a look-and-feel that perfectly fits the topic of and the brand behind the community.

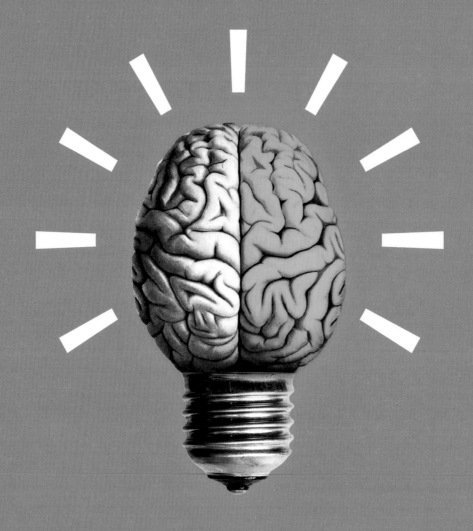

Confessions of a
qualitative mind

by Hakim Zemni

Let me start by presenting myself. I am **Hakim Zemni**. In the companies I have worked for I was often referred to as an *'opinion on legs'*. Personally, I prefer the description *'the guy who doesn't like to leave a question unanswered'*. Currently I am the Managing Director of InSites Consulting's Belgian office, which basically means I make sure we reach our targets and keep our people happy and smart whilst doing so.

Since 1998, by sheer coincidence and luck (the latter being something I'll only realize later), I stumbled into the market research industry. I actually started off as a call center agent to pay for my studies, in a small and local market research agency; pretty soon I was offered a job as a call center supervisor. A few months later I was given the opportunity to become one of the project managers in charge of quantitative studies. Personally, being a communication scientist, my affinity with words has always been way higher than with numbers, but I learned a lot in those first 2 years of working in a quantitative context. But deep down I felt I was a qual mind in a quant body.

In 2000 I shifted from quant to qual and became a full-time qualitative market researcher. Between 2000 and 2008 I conducted 250+ focus groups, 200+ in-depth interviews, gave 100+ workshops and lead 50+ brainstorms. By 2006 I even started a qualitative and independent spin-off within the company I was working for and we actually succeeded in doubling our turnover in a few months' time.

But in 2008 everything changed. To make a long story short, our company was taken over by an international market research company for which I didn't feel any love and from which I didn't feel any passion. So I literally resigned a few hours after the announcement of the buy-out.

What to do then? I had heard about InSites Consulting throughout my 10 years of market research experience and always had a knack for their sexy and dynamic look and feel, their knowledge of the Internet in all its complexity and their academic background. So I gave them a call and introduced myself as a qualitative 'expert'.

What do you think is the future of qualitative research?

September 2008. There I sat, in a room, together with 2 qualitative InSites Consulting seniors. We had a great talk, got on really well from the start. We clicked. The only hiccup in that talk however was rather crucial. **Magali Geens**, then Senior Qualitative Consultant - and today one of the Managing Partners - asked me *'What do* *you think is the future of qualitative research?'*. I gave well-informed and on-topic answers and elaborated on new presentation techniques, ethnography, netnography and web-scraping, doing research without asking questions, life-caching through up-and-coming social media and even talked about ongoing qualitative panels. All of those answers were not wrong, but of course the InSites Consulting people had something else in mind. I kept guessing and guessing, but in vain. In the end they felt sorry for me desperately trying to find the answer they were looking for. The answer was actually just around the corner: *'The future of qualitative research is online'*, they stated. I was shocked in disbelief. I couldn't but counter it. This idea was way too disruptive for a qualitative mind like me. These people were undermining what I did for 10 years, so I told them online qual might be interesting to explore but would never replace focus groups. What about face-to-face contact? What about actually seeing your consumer? What about non-verbal communication? What about the role of the moderator? What about clients wanting to follow groups/interviews? How to convince clients who do not know or realize online qualitative actually exists? I was digging my own grave in the discussion as I kept going on and on and on about the disadvantages high-lighting my skepticism. Luckily, I must have done something right, because 2 weeks later I got offered a contract.

The first weeks

And that is how it all started for me and the online qualitative experience. I started with a research community for a public service broadcaster for which I had already done a lot of offline work before. I felt like a fish on dry land, but much to my surprise I was transferring my offline qual skills quite naturally to the online world from the start. In week one already I remember telling my wife I felt the job was the same, only the medium had changed and the junior qualitative people knew more than me this time around. When analyzing and reporting the findings I even felt I had already been doing it for years. Which is exactly the point of course: analyzing data from a (sometimes poorly) transcribed focus group is in no ways different from analyzing data from a conversation in an online community. Very soon, I felt we were meeting the client's expectations. My comfort zone was literally put to the test but I felt little to no resistance to organically embed the online methods in it.

Converted in 8 weeks

By the end of the first quarter at InSites Consulting my skepticism had become passion, my suspicion had turned into

Hakim Zemni

me as a radical change from what I was used to. I particularly became a fan of the possibility of the holistic approach online qualitative offers: you can ask people to upload pictures and videos, track what they are doing, give them long-lasting assignments, ask them to ponder upon something and work with them on a learning curve, ask them to go on a shopping safari or ask them the traditional qualitative questions at the same time. To me, it all felt like a revolutionary set of techniques in addition to the traditional ones I was able to keep.

The future is here

Today, I am a true believer of Consumer Consulting Boards as the most efficient and meaningful connection one can make with consumers today. I feel lucky that I am part of this paradigm shift as my conviction today is very simple: 70 years ago the focus group was invented as it was the most natural way to ask consumers why and how they did what they did. In the 21st century the online way is the most natural way. With this change of medium we have unlocked a whole new world of qualitative techniques and practices enabling us to not leave any question unanswered. And coincidentally, that's what makes me personally happy.

belief. At that point, early 2009, I started realizing the incredible opportunities ahead for online qualitative. Yes, I was converted and it only took 8 weeks (and a new breed of great *online only* qualitative consultants). Together with my fellow colleagues I started evangelizing the online qualitative word. I talked about unseen advantages such as user-friendliness and convenience for the 21st-century qualitative participant and going beyond the classic 2-to-3-hour consumer connection limit. The disappearance of social desirable answers thanks to the *anonymity* of online tools struck

How different
stakeholders experience
structural collaboration

by Anouk Willems, Natalie Mas & Thomas Troch

In one of the previous articles, the experts stated that a lot of companies have already made a good start with structural collaboration, but no company is there 100% yet. In this article, we will explore what it takes to make structural collaboration a success and how to motivate both the consumer and stakeholders at the company side to keep the spirit of collaboration alive.

Building equal relationships

In order for a Consumer Consulting Board to be successful, it is crucial that an equal relationship between all parties - consumer, company and moderator/researcher - is established and that they see each other as true partners. This particularly holds for research communities, more than in other more traditional research methods. Participants are empowered to start their own discussions and provide the sponsoring company with both solicited and unsolicited feedback, facilitated by the moderator of the community. In order to collaborate and build a strong relationship, companies and researchers need to move away from the traditional research model and shift towards a new model on 3 levels:

1. **Research is not a secret anymore:** The relationship between the company, researcher and consumer should be based on openness, transparency and honesty. When the company is willing to share its own challenges and thoughts, consumers are more motivated to keep on participating. As an example, the marketing manager of **ING** shared his feedback on ideas generated by a community with students around banking, revealing also some of the findings of previous research to show the bigger picture. This openness makes it easier for community members to understand the situation and triggers them to think along and help the manager. The same goes for the moderator: if he/she is more open and shares personal stories, this will set the example for members and it will also put them at ease. For instance, we often ask members to share videos and photos of their homes. In the **Unilever** *R&D community*, we saw it really helps if the moderator also shows his/her place and shares some personal stories. Members feel more safe and triggered to show their own place. Overall, a relationship based on openness will lead to more authentic and valuable contributions.

2. **It's not only about asking questions:** The best relationships are based on active listening. Apart from asking questions and observing, the company and the facilitating researcher both need to show that they are truly listening. Only then the participants will feel like their contributions are worth the effort.

In the *Marktplaats community* (Marktplaats is a member of the **eBay Classifieds Group**), users started sharing some great personal buyer & seller stories in the lounge room, the room on the community where they can start new discussions themselves. Some of these stories were highlighted and praised by the leader of the project at eBay in the monthly update towards the community members. It shows that the company is listening and values the contributions. In the end, it will lead to even more unsolicited feedback and answers to questions the client did not even have.

3. **From *pay* to *play* for attention:** Motivate the community members with intrinsic factors rather than with money rewards. For example: fanatic clubbers are much more interested in unlocking a sneak preview of **Heineken**'s *Club of the Future*, rather than in a money reward. Using elements of gamification to create an engaging experience will lead to more active participation and sincere contributions. This principle also holds for people on the company side. The research manager at H.J. **Heinz** Netherlands prefers to invite marketers to play a game to test their consumer knowledge on a specific topic, rather than to simply share a static report. By sharing inspiration from the Consumer Consulting Board in a fun and engaging way, more employees want to be involved and join the collaboration initiative.

Why consumers want to collaborate with brands

From our *Social Media around the World* study,[21] we learned that more than 4 out of 5 consumers want to collaborate with companies they like, about topics they have affinity with. Consumers like to collaborate with companies in an intimate online environment that offers real interaction with the brand, such as the Consumer Consulting Board. In order to approach these consumers in the right way, we need to appeal to the right motivations.

Shaking the engagement cocktail

To keep all members engaged, we need to create the perfect mix of intrinsic and extrinsic motivators. Intrinsic motivation implies that members contribute for no reward other than the interest and enjoyment that accompanies the activity. In contrast, extrinsic motivation implies that the reason for participating is something other than an interest in the community itself.[22] In addition to these intrinsic and extrinsic motivators, social norms play an important role in online virtual communities. Certain members participate based on more self-centered reasons such as vouchers, where they seek financial benefits for themselves. Other members might feel morally obliged to participate and help the brand, they receive satisfaction from the fulfillment of their community tasks.[23] The following framework shows how the key dimensions group the main ingredients for the cocktail of engagement.

	For myself / me	For others
Intrinsic	1. Interest, enjoyment & curiosity	2. Impact 3. Sense of belonging
Extrinsic	4. Financial rewards	5. Need for status & recognition

The cocktail of engagement

1. **Make it interesting and fun!**
   Members want to talk about topics they are interested in. From the previous part (Bringing consumers into the business, all the way up to the boardroom) we know it is best to invite people that are interested & interesting because they are the ones who keep on participating and at the same time stimulate our thinking and inspire us. Community managers need to play upon this element by enabling members to share their passions with each other. An example: empower them to start sharing their tips and tricks. In the **DE Master Blenders** *Coffee Corner community*, this resulted in sparking discussions about creative coffee recipes, practical tips for coffee to go, newsflashes about coffee &

health and tips on how ground coffee powder is the universal remedy for various household problems. By playing on their shared interests, members learn new things about their favorite topic. Furthermore, by mixing different questioning techniques such as brainstorms, polls and battles, the community manager can trigger curiosity for what will happen next. An illustration: on the same community we post a weekly challenge that invites members to various tasks ranging from becoming an observer for a week and reporting back on how their family/friends consume coffee, or trying out 2 new coffee products and share their experiences, or going on a supermarket safari to analyze the coffee shelves.

....

'I'm a member of the 'Coffee Corner' community. This community is so much fun! As the name suggests, we talk a lot about coffee. I happen to be a real coffee lover :-). It's interesting to read the different opinions and ideas of other coffee lovers. And the topics are always a surprise, which keeps it exciting for me!'

Joke37 of Walk the Talk[*]

....

* Walk the Talk community is set-up by our ForwaR&D Lab. It is a community we created to collaborate with experienced community members and the InSites Consulting community team to evaluate and co-create the future of Consumer Consulting Boards

2. **Empower them:** Participants want to feel that they have had an impact on the brand or the company. The representative of the company, who we call the *ambassador*, needs to speak to the community participants, tell them what they learned and which actions will be taken based upon the input of the Board. Over the past years we learned that participants are realistic: they know that you cannot tell them everything, that some things cannot be implemented because there is no fit with the company's strategy or that it simply takes time to change things within big companies. In the end it is all about managing the expectations towards participants from the beginning, during the kick-off session. A nice example here is the *Wall of fame* we built for the community we

Walk the Talk community

run for H.J. Heinz. This is a separate section on the platform, which showcases all products and campaigns that our members worked on. This *Wall of fame* is a great way to make their impact tangible.

3. **Create a sense of belonging:** Participants want to make new friends. They want to connect with like-minded people and learn more about them. All members have a shared goal they want to reach together. The moderator needs to emphasize this goal to create a group feeling and make participants feel proud to be part of this group. This type of feedback was shared on the *Marktplaats community*. The group was given a challenge to reach 1,000 posts in one week. As a consequence, members started to work together to reach this goal. When they reached the milestone, they even started thanking each other for the great work. Their group efforts were rewarded with feedback from the company including a sneak peek behind the scenes of their office, showing all the teams involved in the

74

....

'The brand should try to address the target group in a transparent way.
The brand has to open up and be somewhat vulnerable so that we actually get the feeling we are also part of the company.'

Ljm_angel69 of Walk the Talk

....

'All the members gather in the community and have a sense of belonging, which I think is very important. And with sense of belonging I mean that we all have the same goal, but still each individual has his or her own opinion.'

Hemeltje of Walk the Talk

....

creation of the new Marktplaats platform. In addition to the group feeling between participants, we also emphasize the sense of belonging among participants and the company. To illustrate, at the start of an online chat session with the brand, we introduced all internal stakeholders involved at **PepsiCo Turkey** to the *Ruffles community* participants. By doing this, the members feel closer to the company and the people behind the brand.

PepsiCo Turkey Team

4. **Reward them with incentives:** While extrinsic rewards with a monetary value are not the main reason for staying engaged on the community, our research-on-research has shown that this type of incentive still needs to be added to our cocktail. When members receive their first invitation mail to join the community, this monetary incentive is considered to be very important. However, as soon as the community has kicked off, we notice a shift in motivations. Members get hooked to the community; the weekly challenges and the feedback they receive from the moderator and the company keeps them energized and motivated to continue. But the monetary reward is not in proportion anymore with the amount of time spent.

....

'Although it is not about the reward in the first place, I do think this is a nice encouragement to participate in a community. In my opinion, the ideal reward would be a surprise package of a certain value. But a gift voucher that can be used anywhere is also nice'

Vincent1 of Walk the Talk

....

75

When members are only motivated by tangible rewards, it will put them in the reward mindset. They link their behavior to the anticipation of the reward. This does not trigger rich data and rapidly reduces activity. Therefore, it is crucial to avoid this type of motivation becoming dominant at all times and this once again confirms why we need to work with people who feel a high topic and/or brand identification. The monetary reward is often handed out as vouchers.

Next to vouchers, the rewards can also be related to the topic of the community or even be part of the research. For example, a community for a national newspaper rewards active members with free subscriptions for a whole year. To the beauty lovers in the Unilever R&D community *Skin Beauty*, we sent goodie bags with the newest skin care products which had only just been launched onto the market. Previous experiments have taught us that most members prefer to receive these kind of topic- or brand-related rewards (56%) rather than to receive a generic voucher (44%).*

5. **Give them recognition and status:** Besides monetary incentives, non-monetary returns are part of the cocktail, such as the status and recognition members receive from the community. The gratification from a successful performance of the participant's role motivates members to participate. Members

like to feel appreciated for their efforts. They want to be recognized as an expert on the topics they are passionate about. For example, when a member posts a great idea that sets an example for the other members, they should be rewarded with an expert badge for making a high-quality contribution.

....

'When I got my expert badge, I bragged to my kids. It's not often we get called such things so why shouldn't we be just pleased with ourselves'

DeeDee of Unilever's InspireUs community

....

Why companies value structural collaboration with consumers

The success of structural collaboration is not guaranteed with an enthusiastic bunch of consumers alone. The internal stakeholders at the company also need

---

* We did an experiment among the community members of the H.J. Heinz Food community (n=141), exploring their preferences regarding incentives: brand-related (goodie bags, new products, branded presents) vs. non-brand related (money vouchers).

to work on maintaining the relationship. Today, 83% of decision makers indicated that they have a research community or that they want to build one this year.[24] The popularity of the method is explained by clients in 3 key benefits: it is flexible, inspiring and impactful.

Flexible: it is a direct consumer line

Contrary to traditional qualitative methods, the Consumer Consulting Board is organized on an online closed platform in an asynchronous way. This enables all stakeholders to be involved in a flexible and efficient way, crossing the boundaries of space and time. **Charles Hageman** from **KLM** considers this a real success factor: *'The key to success of our community is that the internal clients are involved and stay connected throughout the project. In our project, the internal client was involved with the community from the first moment of the kick-off and onwards'.*

Clients experience the community as a flexible and fast gateway to the world of the consumer. They can use it for a wide range of questions and for things they would otherwise not have done research for. **Joella Marsman**, in charge of the community at H.J. Heinz in the Netherlands explains: *'One of the key reasons why our marketers like to collaborate with the community is because it's flexible. When they post a question, they receive almost instant feedback. The community is a very accessible research tool. It is easy for marketers to check with the community members if they are on the right track in different stages of the product development process.'*

Inspiring: it brings the consumer to life

A Consumer Consulting Board generates richer, more accurate and authentic data which is closer to the real-life situation. The long-term connection enables clients to observe the consumer over time. They can also see the less frequent consumer behavior and capture the whole context that is relevant for understanding the consumer. **Tom Armstrong** of **Vodafone** values this bigger picture: *'An increasing number of teams is no longer interested in one particular topic, but more in the overall contextual information, how their target groups are thinking. They're starting to see the benefits of listening to the consumer and integrating that more in their discussions. It brings their consumer to life'.*

77

Next to this 360° view, the internal stakeholders start to feel connected with their consumers. **Leo de Groot**, Program manager at **SBS Broadcasting NL**, was excited about the impact of their community: *'Through the community, we felt really connected with this group of very interested yet critical consumers. There is no more powerful mirror imaginable than getting feedback from them. No longer is their vision 'voluntary' as it is in normal 'focus groups'. The results surely have a direct impact on the choices we make. The conclusions are the wallpaper of our offices.'*

H.J. Heinz Netherlands Food Community team

Impactful: it is a fresh way of working

The structural nature of a Consumer Consulting Board allows for a customized approach that fits with the company's culture, internal processes and business planning. It brings forth a new way of working. The long-term connection enables both members and internal stakeholders to think and re-think their contributions over time and build on previous learnings. **Carole Lamarque** at **bpost** considers the community of real added value to their way of working: *'It's not the snapshot of the questions that has an impact, but it is the co-creation which provides the key benefit: you collaborate with the consumer for a longer period of time. This enables answers to mature over time. And that is what I sometimes miss in research: you just ask someone a question while there's no time to think or talk about it with friends and family. Your environment also has an influence.'*

Besides the iterative approach, we must also think about the format in which the results are shared. Most internal stakeholders like to receive short updates in an easily accessible format that helps them stay in touch with the Consumer Consulting Board. In that way they receive inspiration on a frequent basis that is still manageable. Lamarque continues: *'I think the way to present and diffuse the community results is key. It should almost be like those small magic boxes from McDonald's, with all the helpful tools in there such as results, stories and quotes'.*

Building on the results and inspiration from the Board, internal stakeholders start asking new questions and together they help grow the value of the community over time. **Martijn van Kesteren**, former CMI manager of *Ben & Jerry's* and other Unilever Refreshment brands, experienced this as well: *'My colleagues and I were highly involved with the community, constantly following all the new updates. This made the research really come to life. The results were received with open arms and we translated them into actions. It was great to see that this led to more questions, so we could continue the collaboration and feed the funnel of the discussions'.*

The ambassadors of the communities, such as Martijn van Kesteren and Carole Lamarque, play an important role in growing the value of the community over time. They are the voice of the community. They collect all the questions and challenges of the organization. And they know which internal stakeholders should be involved at what time. Some ambassadors want to fully experience the consumer dialogue as part of the immersion and take the collaboration one step further. At **Alpro**, Unilever and H.J. Heinz for example they wanted to talk to the consumers directly as a co-moderator of the community. They were trained by the *InSites Consulting Moderator Academy* to become community managers and received weekly coaching to develop their community management skills.

The immersion also works the other way around. The community managers from *InSites Consulting* immerse themselves in the company in order to help the ambassador with the right positioning of the community. By being physically present in the office and talking to different internal stakeholders on a regular basis, they get a better understanding of the organization, its culture and the daily struggles. When the advertising agency *Famous* launched its ongoing community, the project team worked at the company for a week, to fully understand their needs. Still today, our community manager regularly works

from the Famous offices to join strategic and creative brainstorms. These immersion efforts help grow the relationship between all parties involved and truly make the community co-owned.

Everybody Famous community workshop

Growing the relationship

When we moved on to the new research model, shook the cocktail of engagement and inspired the internal stakeholders, we laid the foundation for a great relationship between the 3 parties. However, it does not stop here. We must keep on investing in the relationship by sharing company challenges on an ongoing basis. The community is not a one-off project; it is part of the organization. Through this solid relationship, our clients are in a unique position to make a difference within their company and leverage the collaboration with the consumer internally and externally.

79

Recognition
by the industry

Over the past years, InSites Consulting has been endorsed by the marketing research industry with more than 25 national and international awards.

We are proud to showcase the awards and nominations we received for our expertise and work in the field of research communities.

Nominated for

- ESOMAR Best Case History Award 2012 with Heineken
- ARF Great Mind Award 2012 in the category Rising Star for Tom De Ruyck
- MOA Innovation Award 2012 with RTL
- Finalist Forrester Groundswell Award 2012 with Heineken
- Finalist NGMR Award 2010 & 2011 in the category Disruptive Innovator for Tom De Ruyck
- ESOMAR Research Effectiveness Award 2011 with Unilever R&D
- ESOMAR Congress 2011 Best Methodology Award with Unilever R&D
- ESOMAR 2011 Excellence Award with Danone

2010 Awards

- AMA **4 under 40: Marketing Research Emerging Leader Award** 2010
  Tom De Ruyck

- ESOMAR **Online Research Congress Best Paper Award** 2010
  Synergizing natural and research communities with Danone by Annelies Verhaeghe, Tom De Ruyck & Niels Schillewaert

2011 Awards

- CCA **Co-Creation Award** 2011
  Heineken Open Design Exploration project

- Research Live **#MRX Tweeter of the Year Award** 2011
  @tomderuyck

2012 Awards

- MOA **Innovation Award** 2012
  Applying Gamification to research communities by our ForwaR&D Lab team

- CMO Council Asia & USA **Leadership Award for Contribution to Market Research** 2012
  Tom De Ruyck

- Design & Emotion **Best Presentation Award** 2012
  Heineken Nightlife Journey of Clubbers to develop a visionary concept club by Thomas Troch

- ESOMAR **3D Congress Best Presentation Award** 2012
  The use of mobile in Online Research Communities by Annelies Verhaeghe & Anouk Willems

From co-creation to structural collaboration

TWEETAWAYS

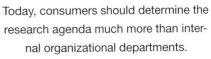

Today, consumers should determine the research agenda much more than internal organizational departments.
@tomderuyck

Diffusing research results should be like getting those small magic boxes from McDonald's, blending results, stories and quotes.
@caroberry

Consumers act as the ideal co-researchers, filling researchers' blind spots as they are not living all those different lives.
@Niels_InSites

70 years ago the focus group was the most natural way to ask consumers about the *why* and *how*. Today, online is the most natural way.
@HakimZemni

Research moves from *pay* to *play* for attention: participants are in it for social reasons, fun & to have a say in the future of brands.
@kristofdewulf

3

**Shaping
your business
through
consumers**

Solving business challenges by **reaching out** to consumers

by Thomas Troch, Annelies Verhaeghe & Anouk Willems

A recent article in *Harvard Business Review* claimed that companies are more able to solve all their main business problems when collaborating closely with their consumers.[1] User contribution can tackle challenges from the technical to the artistic. The emblematic example of contribution in R&D is open source software, such as the *Linux operating system* and the *Mozilla Foundation's Firefox web browser*, which is created and regularly upgraded by communities of unpaid developer volunteers. It is not only efficient to look outside the organization for collaborators; it also proves to be effective. In a compilation of studies of 1,193 commercially successful innovations across nine industries by MIT's **Eric von Hippel**,[2] 737 (60%) came from consumers. One can only imagine the success if organizations and consumers actually join forces, instead of generating ideas separately.

Companies can swiftly provide answers to the changing needs of their consumers by being more open and agile. Although these characteristics are valued any time, there is a sense of urgency to aspire these in order to survive in a time in which new competitors can show up and challenge your business model any day. As consumers are more connected than ever before, competitors can also show up from anywhere in the world and reach your consumers. Close collaboration with consumers improves the performance of organizations as it allows them to make better informed decisions more rapidly. As **Marc Pritchard**, CMO of **P&G**, summarizes; *'The power of everyday people is driving monumental change'*. Traditionally the voice of the consumer is only integrated at the very end of a decision-making flow, missing out on the opportunity to fail faster and iterate together with stakeholders.

Co-creating new products and services is one of the highlights of such collaboration; but the practice moves beyond innovation. Consumers are willing to take up different roles to help companies - from being a judge and helping to improve the proposition to being a peer and sharing their daily live - allowing you to collaborate on four key business objectives, incorporating activities from branding and communication to innovation.

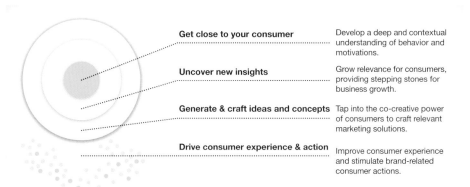

Get close to your consumer
Develop a deep and contextual understanding of behavior and motivations.

Uncover new insights
Grow relevance for consumers, providing stepping stones for business growth.

Generate & craft ideas and concepts
Tap into the co-creative power of consumers to craft relevant marketing solutions.

Drive consumer experience & action
Improve consumer experience and stimulate brand-related consumer actions.

Key business objectives of structural collaboration

While an ad hoc research project typically combines one of these objectives with one specific project or department, the structural element in a Consumer Consulting Board allows you to tap into multiple objectives in different consecutive or parallel waves and continuously build further on previous learnings.

1. Get close to your consumer

How well do you know your consumer? Consumer centricity is a corporate value many organizations share, but the differentiator lies in how the consumer is brought to life within the company. To enhance the consumer feeling of a department, a plant or a complete company and provide a solid outside-in perspective, the Consumer Consulting Board takes a 3-step approach to change the hearts, mind and actions of the team; *engage*, *inspire* and *activate*. Everything starts with the careful selection of the target group, typically people with a very high involvement with your brand and/or with the category. To de-

velop a deep, longitudinal and contextual understanding of their behavior and motivations, it is recommended to apply a mix of ethnographic and conversational techniques. Let's illustrate the 3-step approach with a case for Unilever.

- Engage: creating
  eye-opening experiences

The key to change is engagement; this is the first step in getting close to your consumers. To engage with the consumer world, a traditional research report will not do the trick. We need to confront employees with real people, their real stories and emotions, not only with facts and figures. As a contrast to factual information, we linked each of the Unilever R&D employees to one individual consumer. Over a period of 3 weeks, R&D employees had to play 3 games with questions about the life of the specific consumer they were connecting with. Whilst playing the game, they unlocked the right answers to the questions and

CASE ....

**Changing the hearts, minds
and actions of Unilever R&D**

Unilever

In order to effectively share the rich output from a Consumer Consulting Board in the organization, internal communication is key, both online and offline. **Unilever** was one of the front runners in setting up consumer connect programs. Unilever asked its R&D workforce managers to get out there and engage with the consumer, in order to experience their everyday lives. When the focus of their R&D plant in Vlaardingen (NL) shifted from laundry to beauty products, there was a need to immerse into the beauty habits of their consumers. But how does one entail a positive disruption in a complete R&D plant? ▢

additional information about their consumer, which helped them to do even better in the next consumer game. Competitions between different teams and the eye-opening experience of connecting with individual people made the initiative the talk of the Unilever town.

- Inspire: filling knowledge gaps

To be inspired and gain fresh knowledge, the results of the game and the detected information gaps were guiding the discussions of the Consumer Consulting Board. The results were analyzed on-the-go and featured in crisp articles on a news website, available to the whole R&D organization. At any moment in time, employees were able to share their questions, which were featured on the consumer community to provide an additional level of depth and knowledge to the output.

- Activate: putting into action

As a round-up, final workshops were organized in each department to share learnings and discuss how they should be turned into concrete actions for the future. In this stage we also conducted a post-survey to measure the impact of the study in terms of perceived consumer knowledge and usage levels of the study. The results were compared to those of a pre-test we conducted before the actual start of the project. The activation phase is not only about turning the findings into ac-

tion, but also ensures the outcome of the research to have an afterlife. The ideation with frequent flyers and the **Air France and KLM** team, for example, resulted in 32 new transfer concepts. By spreading these in the format of a printed card deck, the team has a tangible deliverable to use when reviewing their service and communication at regular intervals.

2. Uncover new insights

With the abundance of data currently available to anyone, turning data into insights is what really matters. What sets an insight apart from an observation is its fresh and new character, its relevance for the consumer and a desire to improve the current situation. A Consumer Consulting Board facilitates a unique multi-staged approach for insight activation, maximizing chances to detect strong and differentiating insights. Insights generated through research communities have proven to be 82% more effective in the market.[3] Once the insights are available, their relative strength and potential is assessed through an in-depth quantitative screening procedure. Multimedia ethnography allows the members of the Board to share their experience and habits through stories, pictures and videos on a private and personal blog. The meaningful observations from this blogging stage can then be further shaped in the discussions. Insights are not only vital to inspire innovation, they are also crucial in shaping brands that are relevant to

89

consumers. Take a brand like *J&B*; the insight that lays at the basis of innovation and communication concepts for the brand is: *'In a world of day-to-day constraints and social pressure, consumers want nights out that offer the promise that the unexpected can happen'.* This insight is clearly present in campaigns such as the *Start a Party* initiative, launching parties all over the world at unusual locations from the unfinished *World Cup Stadium* in Cape Town to the *forbidden city* in Beijing.

The blog stories and forum discussions are analyzed through info structuring and pattern detection while visual analysis principles provide understanding of the visual output. But to get everything out of the data, the perspective of the researcher is not enough. By embedding a crowd interpretation game in the platform, participants are presented with the observations from their peers

and are asked to analyze them with the research questions in mind. They take these observations in three levels from a description and an interpretation to an insight. After the analysis, the original contributor of the post can evaluate the interpretation and provide additional feedback. Crowd interpretation is a powerful mechanism: it helps shed new light on the data and delivers 20% to 40% complementary insights which are of a similar quality to the ones derived from researchers.[4]

By involving both the participants and the H.J. Heinz team in the analysis through such a crowd interpretation game, we got a holistic perspective on the data resulting in more and better insights. In addition, this approach also made the insight activation project more visible for H.J. Heinz. It stimulated their thinking as it tested their expertise in consumer know-how and also

90

CASE ....

CASE: Activation and deprivation of Heinz ketchup consumption

When H.J. Heinz was in need for insights on ketchup and cold sauce usage for the front end of their innovation funnel, this was exactly the road they took. Four different groups of consumers in their online community were involved: Heinz ketchup users, consumers who use ketchup but not Heinz, people who use other cold sauces and people who typically use ketchup out of home but do not buy it for in-home consumption. All participants were asked to report on personal and family usage of ketchup and cold sauces. In order to reveal consumers' latent motivations, we organized activation and deprivation exercises. During activation, people were asked to start using ketchup more often. During deprivation periods, they couldn't consume any ketchup for a couple of days and had to report about the moments when they missed it. ☐

tapped into their inherent competitive-
ness as the game virus hit. **Mariken
Kimmels**, H.J. Heinz Marketing Director
Continental Europe, described it as follows in an e-mail to her team:

....

*'I really encourage all of you to
spend this hour as it is not only a
crucial part of the process to get
your thoughts and thinking on
this, but it is also a fun learning
experience for yourself. I just
finished it myself and consider
the time well spent, despite
my busy schedule. Maybe this
is another incentive: I guess
none of you want me to win this
game... :-)'*

**Mariken Kimmels,
Marketing Director Continental
Europe, H.J. Heinz Company**

....

Consumers increasingly expect organizations to involve them in defining their
future. By collaborating with them in the
product, campaign or brand development flow, you create a sort of self-ful-
filling prophecy. Not every consumer is
fit to co-create. Nothing new there. Eric

Crowd interpretation game with consumers and marketers

von Hippel already coined the notion of
leading-edge users in the 80's.[5] Lead
users sense needs before the entire
market does and they are interested in
finding a solution for them. For innovation research it is advisable to approach
consumers who are among the first to
try new products and are prepared to
take a risk with it. But while we need a
group of innovators, diffusion of innovations happens when an innovation is
*'communicated through certain channels
over time among the members of a social
system'.*[6] Based on theories from social
psychology and innovation adoption we
therefore add a dimension to our ideation and development approach: *social
independence* versus *interpersonal influence*. As such we propose two complementary types of consumers to ideate
and develop concepts within a certain
product category:

- **Independent innovators** These
  people formulate their vision about
  an innovation independently. They

91

base this vision solely on their own experience and opinions, without taking into account what might be popular. They like to try new things and generally have more extreme views than the average consumer.

- Social influencers: This group discusses innovations whilst taking into account what their social environment thinks. Influencers are regarded as creative specialists, who are quick to see the advantages of new innovations. Consequently, their opinions about such innovations are frequently asked for - and followed.

To generate new ideas, develop concepts and optimize go-to-market strategies for products and services, it is not enough to select consumers with the right profile. They are not only there to generate solutions for the problems they encounter. They should generate solutions that are relevant to a wider audience, based on their experience. Inspire them with specific insights that already exist in the company or that follow from a previous research wave to reach this point of relevance. The strengths of the co-created concepts and products can be validated through a sequential and integrated innovation flow from idea screening to concept testing and in-home user testing.

4. Drive consumer experience & action

A great or even wowing consumer experience is the best guarantee for future success. Even when you start from validated consumer insights and co-create solutions with your community, there are still a lot of variables to get right between defining the proposition and launching a product,

CASE

**Air France and KLM
co-create the future transfer
experience with frequent flyers.**

The frequent flyers in the Consumer Consulting Board of Air France and KLM are having a major impact on the new transfer experience vision of both airline companies. In consecutive waves they explored frictions in the current customer experience and discovered insights, which were later used to brief another group of frequent travelers to generate new ideas together with the Air France and KLM team. In complex situations like transfers, where different stakeholders (travelers, airline, airport, security and customs) come together, putting the consumer at the center of the marketing process unites and engages all parties into anticipating consumer needs. Read more about this case on page 108.

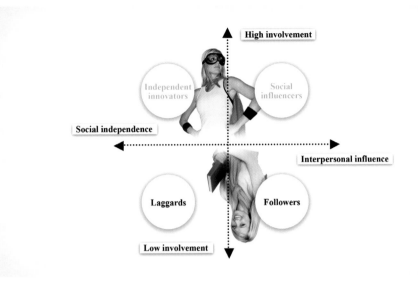

User types of product/service innovations

service or campaign to the market. Therefore getting the prototype or solution out of the lab as soon as possible is important in order to understand the actual consumer experience. From pre-launching a service to exploring the shopper journey and continuously improving existing services, consumer challenges and conversations allow you to assess and develop a delightful customer experience. The final goal is to drive the actions of consumers: talking about your brand, recommending

93

CASE ....

Smartphone users get exclusive access to Vodafone applications before launch.

Vodafone is driving consumer experience and action by involving several communities across Europe in the improvement of their Internet services, with specific attention to first-time smartphone users. By giving consumers exclusive access to these services before launch, they can experience them in a real-life setting. The entire consumer journey related to their different services was mapped in different waves, highlighting triggers and barriers in three core areas: assessing the performance of the service, understanding the emotional resonance in the user experience and defining the go-to-market strategy. The match between the perception of the Vodafone brand and the experience of the service was driving the development of the messaging. In a first phase, the consumer insights inspired the creation of the communication campaign. Next, the Vodafone community shared spontaneous associations on the branding statements before providing feedback on visual mock-ups. The voice of the consumer is thus integrated in all key phases of the branding and communication development to ensure the message resonates with what is important to the target group. Read more about this case on page 118. ▢

products or services and ultimately buying them. By actively looking for elements that are conversational in these research waves, these can be emphasized in the positioning and go-to-market messaging as illustrated in the Vodafone case.

Structural leverage of research

To structurally get the consumer on board, every single day and for almost all decisions that need to be taken, there is a need to develop longer-term connections with them. By moving away from ad hoc interactions, involving the Consumer

Consulting Board can increase both efficiency and effectiveness with the advantages of the consecutive learning effect, building further on learnings from previous waves. The decision on which topics to put on the agenda will increasingly shift from the company to the members of the Board. They like to talk about what's important to them. This is true for all target groups, but particularly for Gen Y as **Joeri Van den Bergh** depicts in chapter 4. As a consequence of this intense collaboration between your company and the market, decisions will no longer be imposed from above. And when the majority of your decisions are taken after consultation with the market, the consumer is truly represented in the boardroom.

CASE ···

Famous creatives get inspired by the everyday life of consumers.

Famous, a Belgian advertising agency, wanted to become the first co-inspiration agency in the world to integrate the voice of the consumer in every stage of the creative process. The Everybody Famous community is giving consumers an active role in advertising. It serves as a window on the target group and provides inspiration in every stage of the campaign development. From emerging trends in society and the adoption of new media and technologies to campaign specific topics, the stories of consumers are at the core of the Famous creative process. This Consumer Consulting Board is completely customized to the activities of the agency, providing 24/7 inspiration and feedback. Even in the most hectic situations such as the moment before a pitch to a client, the strategic team can count on the stories and opinions of their Everybody Famous members by posting 4, 24 or 48 hour challenges depending on the urgency. ▢

Get close to
your consumer

Unilever

Uncover
new insights

Heinz

Business
objectives

Drive consumer
experience & action

vodafone

Generate
& craft ideas
and concepts

KLM AIRFRANCE

The best
consultants
you can
hire?
**Your
consumers!**

by Kristof De Wulf

Unilever's CMO **Keith Weed** gained widespread attention stating *'We must get to the future first'*. The underlying driver for this statement was his realization that consumers are closer to the future than the Unilever organization itself. He was not comparing Unilever with its direct competitors **P&G**, **Henkel** or **Nestlé**, but with consumers… Interesting, don't you think? We think Keith is right.

The conditions for a perfect storm are here. New digital technologies are opening up exciting possibilities to connect with consumers every day, there is increased pressure for brands and organizations to keep up with consumer trends and competition, and consumers are increasingly expecting and even claiming to have a say on the future of 'their' brands. Every day, more consumers are willing and even demanding to co-create and collaborate with brands.

That's why we feel it is of paramount importance to close the gap between organizations and their consumers, driving transparency and connecting both worlds with each other. We believe there is an inherent consulting potential within each consumer that can help organizations drive new and unique added value they may not get to otherwise. Ultimately, the organization of the future reserves a seat on its board for the *Chief Consumer Officer*, acting as the voice of the consumer on the highest possible hierarchical level.

It also implies consumer insights teams need to reinvent themselves. Market research typically is a sort of hatch between consumer and marketer: the researcher listens to the consumer and translates this into what a marketer needs. All too often there is an iron curtain between marketing and consumers. This model is clearly part of the past. The researcher of the future will need to behave more like a coach of both consumer and marketer and facilitate the interaction between them. Researchers and marketers will need to learn to delegate some of their current responsibilities to consumers, not only because the latter expect that more and more, but mainly because they are simply better suited to execute certain tasks than researchers are.

We had the unique opportunity to talk to different senior decision makers and learn from them how they involve consumers in impacting their organizations. Everyone we spoke with touched at least one of the 4 areas in which we feel consumers can make a significant difference for companies.

97

Jörgen Andersson

Mariken Kimmels

Erwin Segers

Gaby Vreeken

Tijn van Elderen

Frank Abenante

1. Getting close

Getting under the skin of users and fans, really understanding what makes them tick and allowing the corporate teams to think, feel and act like them. **Jörgen Andersson**, SVP Director Brand & New Business at **Esprit** and **Mariken Kimmels**, Marketing Director Continental Europe at **H.J. Heinz Company**, share their thoughts on the strategic importance of staying connected and of 'hard listening' to consumers.

Brands for the people by the people

By Jörgen Andersson
SVP Director Brand
& New Business, Esprit

Retrieved from an interview by Joeri Van den Bergh, for his book How Cool Brands Stay Hot: Branding to Generation Y.

Going back to when it all started, in 1968, Esprit was a brand for the people by the people. The democratic movement from that time is very much reflected in the Esprit brand and we think this is even more relevant today. Today's consumers want to be involved in the future of companies and brands, engaging themselves to create that future, but at the same time also coming together as a group, making themselves heard and protesting against what they do not like or consider to be less acceptable. You could even say that, as a result of the unlimited openness and transparency in today's economy, the consumer is the brand and the brand is the consumer. Everything tends to flow together. But reality is lagging behind: the majority of consumers feels left out yet wants to make a difference. Simply pushing your business model to consumers is quite comparable to the arrogance many political leaders in the Middle East are revealing. You will be forced out of power if you are a politician. Consumers will stop buying if you are a company. Relevance is the magic word today. The minute we start taking our partner for granted, the minute we stop listening to them or stop respecting them, will be the beginning of the end. If you stop listening, you stop caring. Becoming and staying relevant requires a continuous and hardcore listening to and collaborating with consumers. That is why the true CEO of any company should be the consumer. We need to tap into consumers' collaborative instincts and engage them in our daily thinking and acting: do they like what we are doing; do they think we should do things differently; what ideas do they have for our brand? If you really start listening to consumers, all the answers are out there. Gather all the answers, take them back to the company, start creating with those as a foundation and give back faster and better than anyone else.

All of this requires brands to open up and go beyond just having a great product or service. Brands need to have a personality which allows them to escape the commodity magnet. Consumers outpace most brands, copying what brands are doing and creating their own new reality from it. Money nor power, nothing stands in their way. If you are talented and creative, you can make it happen. From a pure product perspective, everyone has more or less the same and there is no kind of secrecy in the consumer segment anymore. Why make a distinction between what you tell employees versus consumers? Our internal *Esprit magazine* shared with employees contains more than 80% content that is relevant for consumers as well. Just by opening that up, we can create a whole new range of possibilities.

Finally, the challenge is to never let your dialogue with the consumer fade out. Be prepared to change all the time: the minute you stand still and lean back, someone will be coming after you. Relating it back to personal relationships, most divorces happen when people start taking each other for granted.[7]

ESPRIT

Esprit is an international fashion brand that has been bringing style and quality to life since 1968. Founded in San Francisco by **Susie** and **Doug Tompkins**, Esprit has a creative and responsible DNA fused with a sunny Californian attitude. The Esprit label comprises apparel, footwear, accessories, jewelry and housewares.

Esprit is present in over 40 countries with more than 1,000 directly managed stores and over 10,000 wholesale retailers who share the company's quality standards and brand essence.

by Mariken Kimmels
Marketing Director
Continental Europe,
H.J. Heinz Company

Too many marketers do not realize that the gap between brands and consumers is increasing. We are still focusing too much on making the brand the hero in everything we do. We love talking about our brand and telling consumers what we think is interesting for them and as a result we forget to really listen to them and to be relevant in their lives. In this rapidly changing world fundamentally affecting attitudes and values of our consumers we need to transform our thinking from the brand as the hero to making the individual the hero in everything we do. We have been focusing too much on attracting consumers to our brand world, while we should make our brand present and relevant in their world, in their daily lives. The only way to do so is by making consumers an integrated part of everything we do. That means we need to stop talking about ourselves and start listening.

In order to do so we need to connect with consumers 24/7, not just when we need an insight for a new concept or when we want to tell them something we think they will like about our brand. Truly understanding and being relevant in their world means: being with them and listening to them all the time and using that as the basis for all the deci-

99

sions you have to take as a marketer. As brand owners we all know we need to put the consumers at the heart of our decisions and we claim we are doing that… but are we really? That would mean we have to let go of the control we want to have over our brands and products. Making the individual the hero means that we put them in the driver's seat of our brands… and that is a frightening thought for a marketer, because where does that leave us and our control over the brand? Actually it leaves us in a very powerful place, as with all the new technologies available to us we have all the tools to make our brands relevant in the daily life of people. We are the linking pin between the best consultants you can have, the consumers, and our brands. It is our job to truly connect and bond our brands with everyday consumers in a way that is relevant to them; as a result you will start closing the gap…

The H.J. Heinz Company, headquartered in Pittsburgh, Pennsylvania, is the most global of all USA-based food companies. Famous for its iconic brands on six continents, H.J. Heinz provides delicious, nutritious and convenient foods for families in 200 countries around the world. In more than 50 of those countries, H.J. Heinz Company enjoys the number-one or number-two market position. Throughout the world, Heinz is synonym with ketchup. It sells 650 million bottles of Heinz ketchup and approximately two single-serve packets of ketchup for every man, woman and child on the planet every year. Next to ketchup, H.J. Heinz also markets an ever-expanding selection of other great tasting foods including sauces, meals, snacks, and infant/nutrition. H.J. Heinz employs 32,000 people around the globe.

2. Uncovering insights

Getting to new and relevant consumer insights that allow brands to drive consumer relevance and generate paths for renewed growth. **Erwin Segers**, CMO at **Cloetta** and **Gaby Vreeken**, Global SVP Marketing at **Unilever Food Solutions**, stress the importance of being relevant in today's marketing environment, requiring strong consumer-driven insights as pathways for sustainable long-term growth.

Putting the C back in FMCG

by Erwin Segers
CMO, Cloetta

Social media is not a goal in itself, but is offering us the opportunity to get closer to the consumer and to improve our innovation initiatives and our communication with our consumers. It is an opportunity to put the consumer really at the center of our business. In a world where traditional media is becoming less effective and where trade partners are gaining more power in the relationship with the consumer/shopper, it is crucial for a brand to keep a strong relationship with the consumer in order to maintain and build brand loyalty. When I took on the role of CMO at Cloetta, I decided to use social media to increase consumer centricity. Social media allows us to interact at each step of the purchase funnel and transform funnel thinking into circular thinking. We drafted, designed and implemented a holistic social media strategy delivering value in terms of insight detection, product ideation, customer care handling, brand activation and brand conversations.

Installing our Consumer Consulting Board was a first essential step in our social media journey. Searching for insights that can provide the basis for product ideation was the ambition. In my experience, marketers do not spend enough time and energy in really defining insights. *What is the problem you would like to solve?* A wrong statement concerning a consumer problem or dilemma is often the start of an expensive journey towards market failure. Spending time and energy in generating and validating insights is essential to increase the success of innovation and thus decrease the total product development costs. We were happily surprised to see that brand fans are very open to share their habits and dilemmas, making it a very productive journey

Cloetta

Cloetta, founded in 1862, is a leading confectionery company in the Nordics, the Netherlands and Italy. Cloetta is manufacturing and marketing sugar confectionery, chocolate products, pastilles and chewing gum. In total, Cloetta products are sold in more than 50 markets worldwide. Cloetta owns some of the strongest brands on the market, e.g. Läkerol, Cloetta, Jenkki, Kexchoklad, Malaco, Sportlife, Saila, Red Band and Sperlari, all with a long heritage tradition.

for us. Especially the fact that you are able to connect with your target audience in their own habitat during a longer period is delivering very inspiring and in-depth consumer data.

Next to insight generation, we wanted to tackle the declining ROI of traditional media through social media. As a company grouping multiple brands, we need to be very selective in what we spend our brand communication money on and the contribution it has in reaching our marketing objectives. The huge shift in the way consumers communicate and the role of social media as an accelerator are creating big opportunities. We changed the way we communicate on social media by moving from disruptive communication towards interactive connection, by translating consumer insights into engagement insights and by shifting from heavy-weight campaigns towards a light-weighted but continuous publishing calendar. Using Social Media pilots *(Social Media Speedboats)*, we created spin-off effects for other brands in the commercial organizations. Being successful really requires setting up dialogues with our consumers in a continuous way around topics that are of genuine interest to them.

We need to bring the C back in FMCG. And the best way to do that is by directly involving consumers in what we are trying to achieve as brands. It is not a threat, but the largest opportunity ever, if you do it right.

by Gaby Vreeken
*Global SVP Marketing,
Unilever Food Solutions*

At Unilever Food Solutions, our vision is to support chefs and caterers in satisfying their guests with inspiring, healthy, nutritious food which keeps them coming back for more. In order to deliver against the promise we make of bringing *Inspiration every day*, it is absolutely essential to understand the daily context our clients are operating in and to drive relevance from that. It means that what we do is not only for chefs, but also by chefs. We work closely with chefs and caterers in 74 countries, in order to find the critical balance between impressing guests, to keep up with people's changing tastes, to make a profit and to address important food issues that have been identified by consumers.

Being part of Unilever, we are in a unique position to understand guests and leverage new insights on guests to make a difference for chefs and caterers: our clients. One example of insight sharing is the release of our global authority report on the food service industry. The *What's in Your Food?* report identified the first key industry issue to be addressed by chefs, caterers and the food service industry as a whole: an urgent need for global transparency when it comes to information about food. A key finding in the report shows that 9 out of 10 consumers are demanding more information about food when eating out of home, highlighting the growing need for the food service industry to provide increased transparency for consumers about what is in their food, about where the food comes from and about the safety of the food. Additionally, the majority of people aspire to live healthier lifestyles; however, despite global consensus on the importance of eating healthily, poor levels of information were cited as a significant barrier to leading a healthier lifestyle. As a follow-up to the report, we also launched a concrete service,

Unilever Food Solutions is the food service division of Unilever. Our ingredients are some of the staples of professional kitchens in 74 countries around the world: Knorr, Hellman's, Lipton and more. We provide products that save precious prep time in the kitchen, without compromising on flavor or flair. We've been in food since the 1880s. We're chefs ourselves. So we understand that critical balance between impressing your guests and making a profit. And how to keep your menus and recipes fresh and exciting, as times and tastes change. Unilever Food Solutions is committed to sustainable growth whilst making a positive impact on the food service industry. That means creating healthy, nutritious ingredients using sustainably-sourced packaging that generates less waste. It also means providing services that help chefs and operators run a more sustainable kitchen with healthier menu options for diners.

Seductive Nutrition. Through this service we help our customers to make small changes to their top dishes - making these healthier but still really appealing to consumers.

This is an exciting time for Unilever Food Solutions. We need to keep on collaborating with both food service partners and consumers to provide solutions to real problems, leading the way in actively giving guests what they are demanding.

3. Ideating & crafting

Generating new ideas, co-creating new concepts and refining existing product propositions, thus enabling to better respond to consumer needs. **Tijn van Elderen**, CEO at **Brabantia**, talks about creating real value with real people, not just from within his own organization, but also from outside, co-creating new products with shoppers and consumers.

Creating real value with real people

by Tijn van Elderen
CEO, Brabantia

Marketing has always been good at using TLAs: B2B, B2C, DMU, SKU, WOM, USP and so on. TLA stands for three letter abbreviations. Every time a new guru or organization comes up with a new

term, the whole marketing community runs after the latest TLA.

The latest additions to this field are four letter abbreviations: ZMOT and UMOT. ZMOT of course stands for the Zero Moment of Truth. Whereas in the old days (5 years ago!) shoppers used to trust the corporation selling a product, service or idea, today they only trust people like themselves: other shoppers/buyers who have left information, opinions, references and testimonials about a certain product on the Internet. When shoppers start their (online) search, this is called the ZMOT. The UMOT (Ultimate Moment of Truth) is when the object of their desire has been liked, re-tweeted, filmed etc. as support for the ZMOT.

How does this all affect Brabantia? Shoppers often know more about our products than the salesperson in the

Brabantia has a range of some 1,000 houseware products in five core categories: waste storage, food storage, food preparation, laundry care and hardware, which includes post boxes and bathroom accessories. Since 1919, the company has grown and it now has four production units employing 1,000 employees across 85 countries. In 1919 it was about designing and manufacturing metal products for use around the home - items such as milk sieves, funnels, buckets and watering cans. Today the focus is still on beauty and durability and, through continued and reliable use, also on the understanding that even humble household products can be a pleasure to use and to look at.

103

store, so confidence and reliance on salespeople has decreased. They don't trust our ads. We need other ways to communicate the value of our offering. What it basically boils down to, is that we need to create and communicate real value. Has that not been the principle of doing business successfully since the beginning of times? So maybe nothing has changed at all?! Or has it?

Over the last 94 years, we have seen the up-rise of new media such as magazines, radio, TV and outdoor. The big advantage now is that you can create value together with your shoppers and get instant feedback. At Brabantia, we do this through programs such as creating designs together with our shoppers. We call this activity *Design your bin*. We took the best designs and simply started production. We did the same for our ironing board covers. And we aim to do this more in the future. I don't know of a TLA that covers this. I would suggest a five letter abbreviation: RV-W-RP or *Real Value With Real People*.

4. Activating

Activating consumers to live and report on their experiences, to connect and share brand content with their peer groups and to act as brand ambassadors. **Frank Abenante**, Global VP Brands & Innovation at **AB InBev**, shares different cases, demonstrating

that the communication success does not just depend on strong insights and great creativity, but also to a huge extent on the way consumers are involved and help spread the word.

Frank Abenante
Global VP Brands,
AB InBev

The evolution of the media landscape and the surge in the social media arena have triggered in Anheuser-Busch InBev both a genuine interest and an urgent necessity to revisit the role our brands play in people's lives and the way these brands connect with people. We have fully embraced the concept of *Brand Ideal* or *Brand Purpose*, where every brand needs to enunciate the defining, relevant role it should play in people's lives: the statement that constitutes the guiding compass for the positioning.

In the case of *Budweiser*, that purpose is the championing of opportunity through celebration and optimism. One of the projects aiming at integrating consumers into the story was *Budweiser Project 12*. The idea was to develop a relevant line extension, together with our consumers, that would help generate trial with younger adults while giving our loyal consumer a chance to try *Budweiser* again, as if for the first time. We briefed our 12 *Budweiser Brew Masters* from our 12 breweries in the US. They submitted their best brew, and with the help of consumers in every region, we reduced the list to 6 variants which we subsequently reduced to a final set of 3. Then we launched these 3 liquid variants in a mixed 6-pack, under the *Budweiser Project 12 trademark*, each variant named after their original brewing batch as well as the zip code from the brewery they came from. Consumers voted for their preferred brew during a 4-month period. We entered in a dialogue with consumers that eventually culminated in the selection of the brew from our Los Angeles Brewery, which then became *Budweiser Black Crown*, our most recent national launch under our *Budweiser* brand umbrella.

Another example of consumers fully integrated in our storytelling was *the Clydesdales campaign* around the Superbowl 2013. For years, AB InBev

AB InBev is the leading global brewer, one of the world's top five consumer product companies and recognized as first in the beverage industry on FORTUNE Magazine's 'World's Most Admired' companies list. Beer, the original social network, has been bringing people together for thousands of years and its portfolio of well over 200 beer brands continues to forge strong connections with consumers. Geographically diversified with a balanced exposure to developed and developing markets, Anheuser-Busch InBev leverages the collective strengths of its approximately 118,000 employees based in 23 countries worldwide. In 2012, AB InBev realized 39.8 billion US dollar revenue.

has used these noble animals as symbols of tradition, heritage, strength and resilience. They have always played, in one way or another, a key role during those highly expected Superbowl advertising moments. In 2013, we crafted a beautiful, highly emotional story about the reunion of a *Clydesdale* and his trainer, after some years of separation. Then we took advantage of the fact that 2 foals were born a few days before the Superbowl night, so we released the story prior to the national telecast, asking consumers to vote for their favorite name for the foals. Hundreds of thousands of responses led to the names of STAN and HOPE, which in turn energized our consumer base to search for *Budweiser* and *Clydesdales* on the web, which we subsequently linked to new *Clydesdales* stories they could relate to. And it worked! The 60-seconds *Clydesdales* ad was the most viewed spot on YouTube during the Superbowl, surpassing 15 million views; it achieved 3.5 million views before Superbowl night; it was the 3rd most shared Superbowl ad of all times, with over 2 million shares on Facebook; it was the number one Superbowl ad according to *USAToday AdMeter*; it generated the highest ever search interest over *Budweiser* in the web.

Do not let consumers stand aside; involve them in creating and sharing your brand story. If you get it right, it will pay off big time.

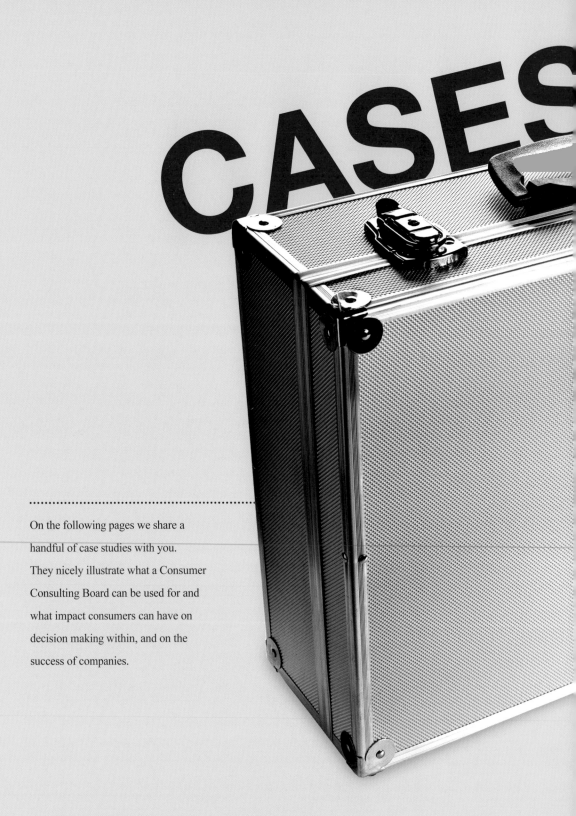

CASES

On the following pages we share a
handful of case studies with you.
They nicely illustrate what a Consumer
Consulting Board can be used for and
what impact consumers can have on
decision making within, and on the
success of companies.

MY TRANSFER INSIGHT ACTIVATION & IDEATION COMMUNITY

In order to further improve the experience of their travelers, the airline companies **Air France and KLM** connected with their frequent flyers on an emotional level, through a staged innovation approach. During this innovation project, Air France and KLM gained insights before developing and validating new concepts to optimize the transfer experience.

Frequent flyers and their stories

As major airlines are fighting a continuous battle for customers in this period of economic uncertainty, Air France and KLM felt the importance of increasing their focus on customer experience as a way to keep existing customers and attract new ones. Transfer flights in particular are perceived as complex and stressful and they evoke a lot of negative emotions. For most travelers, the 'transfer between connecting flights' is a phase in their journey they would be only too happy to skip. Transfer flights are chosen mainly because there is no other option available or when travelers need to make a trade-off between time and costs. This is why it is crucial for airports and airline companies to understand the needs, expectations and emotions of travelers during transfer.

The *My Transfer Idea* Community

In order to turn the current situation into an opportunity and to demystify the innovation process, InSites Consulting and Air France and KLM collaborated with frequent travelers during 6 weeks in a co-creation project. By connecting with 40 frequent flyers in a 3-week Consumer Insight Activation Community, the passengers shared over 400 observations in text and pictures. Their personal blogs allowed us to immerse in the world of transfer. Based on these insights, 10 insight platforms were defined, emphasizing their needs, emotions and expectations.

The insight platforms from the blogging phase were used during the second stage of the *My Transfer Idea* community, where another group of 50 frequent travelers joined forces to generate over 450 ideas and comments

to improve the transfer experience. In this 3-week *Ideation and Concept Development Community* the travelers were stimulated to discuss and build further on each other's initial ideas. Based on the ideas and the community discussion we were able to craft 32 concepts for new transfer services.

In a final phase, the four consumer-generated concepts that were showing the highest business relevance were tested in a quantitative idea screener among a representative sample, capturing not only traditional innovation KPIs but also emotions both in an explicit and an implicit way.

The transfer experience of the future

Three of the final service concepts are currently being investigated by Air France and KLM: a mobile transfer application including real-time consumer notifications and communication about travel details, a new in-flight transfer video and a concept known as *The Agent of the Future*. Furthermore, the insights and the other 29 concepts have laid the blueprint for future service innovations in the transfer zone and many other new initiatives.

The My Transfer Idea community

Presented at the ESOMAR Qualitative Congress 2013 in Amsterdam (NL) and the MIE 2013 event in Den Haag (NL).

109

Shaping your business through consumers

CLUBBERS INSPIRE THE CREATION OF A PROGRESSIVE HEINEKEN NIGHTCLUB

The **Heineken**-sponsored global design project, which went under the title of *Open Design Explorations Edition 1: The Club*, invited 19 emerging designers from around the world to co-create the club of the future. To immerse themselves in the nightlife journey, the design team connected in a Consumer Consulting Board with over 100 design-savvy clubbers.

History meets future

The historical legacy behind Heineken's design credentials is what led the brand to pursue its progressive roots and encourage emerging designers. In 2011, the aluminium bottle, which has since become rather famous, won numerous design prizes - amongst which a *Cannes Lion* - and Heineken is now connecting with design that goes beyond just beer, by enhancing *beer moments* in a unique collaborative project. This way, they can strengthen their position as a premium brand in the world of clubbing and design.

Heineken invited emerging designers from Milan, Sao Paulo, New York & Tokyo to submit their portfolio via Heineken's *Facebook page*. Live presentation events in these four design cities resulted in the final selection of 19 designers from a broad range of backgrounds; product, graphic, fashion, interior and motion design, all joining forces in one and the same challenge: designing the club of the future.

The Heineken *Concept Club* community

To develop a relevant and impactful take on club design, it is crucial to understand the needs of clubbers, which is why *The Heineken Concept Club community* was set up, a 3-week Consumer Consulting Board with 120 design-savvy clubbers in the 20 hottest cities in the world. This inspirational adventure provided the design team with relevant and real consumer insights, acting as a briefing, a source of inspiration and a springboard for ideation. Through discussions, diaries, pictures and videos, these clubbers shared their experiences and the role of clubbing in their routines together with their expectations towards the ideal nightlife journey.

The dialogue with this dynamic target group resulted in over 2,000 comments, providing a unique view on the essence of clubbing.

To engage and inspire the designers with the research results, a customized reporting format was developed. The analysis of the discussions resulted in 28 insights, each linking a challenge for the design team to the needs of their audience. Service-design thinking inspired the integration of these insights – spread over six touchpoints – in a customer journey map that visualized the experiences, needs, perceptions and motivations of the clubbers.

By reporting the consumer journey map as an interactive infographic, the designers could browse through the night and discover the insights in the different phases of a night out, from pre-club drinks and meeting up, to entering the club, going for a drink, dancing, chilling and finally going home.

The Heineken Concept Club

The interactive customer journey map did not only serve as briefing and a source of inspiration; it was also crucial in the final selection of the concepts which became part of the actual club. By taking the journey of clubbers as a starting point, *The Heineken Concept Club*, showcased at the *Milan Design Week 2012*, successfully provided the design critics with a pleasant surprise. From the layout of the club - following the customer journey map - to the shelves where clubbers can leave their drink while dancing, the entire experience was designed to provoke a truly enjoyable and memorable night out. Through initiatives like this, Heineken is setting itself apart by pushing the boundaries of design and by emphasizing design as a key part of their brand DNA.

 Winner CCA Co-Creation Award 2011 and *Best Presentation Award* at the 8th International Conference on Design & Emotion 2012

Presented at the ESOMAR Congress 2012 in Atlanta (US) and the 8th International Conference on Design & Emotion 2012 in London (UK).

111

Shaping your business through consumers

HOW HEINZ CONNECTED CONSUMERS TO THE COMPANY VIA THE FOOD COMMUNITY

In 2008, **H.J. Heinz Netherlands** - famous for its ketchup - was on the lookout for an online qualitative platform which would allow them to quickly tap into consumer feedback to guide day-to-day marketing decisions. Today, this platform has grown into the *Food & Zo Community* (Dutch), a Consumer Consulting Board with 150 consumers who inspire managers from research, marketing, communication and R&D departments on tactical and strategic questions. The goal is to have a direct consumer line that activates managers in the short run and helps shape their consumer feeling to make better decisions faster in the long run.

In search of a direct consumer line

For many years H.J. Heinz Netherlands had been using qualitative and quantitative research methods to gain consumer insights. All of these studies are very useful, but the information is often fragmented and abstract, which made it difficult to improve the employees' feeling with the consumer. H.J. Heinz set the goal to really inspire marketers of the different categories and create one platform where marketers and consumers could be in direct contact, making consumers more tangible and giving marketers a chance to experience consumer reality first hand. This resulted in the ongoing *Food Community*.

The Food Community

This Consumer Consulting Board is centered on or around food, in order to make it relevant for the different brand teams. The members of the *Food Community* share a strong interest in food products and cooking. They are all responsible for the grocery shopping and the majority is female.

To get the best out of the members, we used various tools & techniques to create engaging experiences in the community. For example, one of the key motivators for members is to have an impact on future offerings. Sharing feedback is fundamental to boost this feeling. However, we wanted to make this feedback more explicit. That is why we designed our very own *Wall of Fame* in a separate section of the community. This gallery displays all the products and campaigns that had already been inspired by the community and that our members collaborated on. For example, the recent H.J. Heinz Netherlands product activation campaign for the BBQ season.

Members helped to fine-tune this campaign by making H.J. Heinz understand which promotions were most relevant. By showing the results on our Wall of Fame, the members grow pride in about what they had accomplished together.

From day-to-day decisions to inspiration for strategic projects

The conversation funnel consists of different discussion streams. For instance, the community collaborates with managers on *48h challenges* which are quick ad hoc questions from the executives. They can receive immediate feedback on their plans and ideas, without any set-up costs or a long start-up time. Another example: members are often asked for feedback on different versions of advertisements. These questions - which replace the old *corridor tests* that were often conducted among colleagues - invite consumers to think along instead. This filter helps managers to continue with the most relevant ideas and allocate resources efficiently.

In addition to these short-term decisions, the community is also consulted in bigger strategic projects spread out across multiple weeks. For example, by describing their shopping and cooking routines to us, members help us translate new food trends such as *creative cooking* into relevant concepts and ideas. These discussions are followed by offline workshops with the project team which then translates the insights into actions and next steps. After the workshop, follow-up questions and developed concepts are fed back into the community, enabling executives to collaborate in short iterative loops.

The path towards structural collaboration

Today, teams from multiple departments collaborate with the *Food Community* on a structural basis. In 4 years' time, the community has grown in terms of investment, intensity of usage and also the number of internal stakeholders involved. The *Food Community* is successful in the sense that asking consumer feedback has become part of the marketers' day-to-day practice. More and more executives experience the value of the community. The community ambassador at H.J. Heinz, **Joëlla Marsman** (Market Research Analyst), plays an important role in growing the value of the community over time. Her mission is to ask the right questions and involve the right stakeholders at the right time. She is also a part-time moderator, making the community truly co-owned.

··

Presented at the Merlien Insight Valley Europe Summit 2012 in Amsterdam (NL)

114

The H.J. Heinz Food community

HOW
CONSUMERS
EXPERIENCE
THE IKEA
CATALOGUE

The yearly catalogue is **IKEA**'s main communication channel with existing and potential customers globally. Through Customer Consulting
Boards in five different countries, the *2013
edition of the IKEA Catalogue* was evaluated
around the world.

Evaluating the IKEA Catalogue

The international retailer IKEA has the vision *to create a better everyday life for many people by offering a wide range of well-designed, functional home furnishing products at prices so low that as many people as possible will be able to afford them*. Since 1951, the IKEA Catalogue has been a vital part of IKEA retailing and today, more than 200 million households around the world receive the IKEA Catalogue in their letterbox.

For the 2013 edition, significant changes were made to the format (slightly bigger), content (offering more inspiration pages, including more storytelling and a different way of picturing the products) and structure of the Catalogue. Furthermore, a complementary mobile application was launched. Structural changes that were made that were making it even more important to properly understand people's emotional and rational reactions to the new edition.

In order to maximize the impact of this spearhead touch point, IKEA wanted to assess the perception, satisfaction and engagement level the 2013 IKEA Catalogue evokes. Moreover, they wanted to understand how the IKEA Catalogue can inspire and stimulate home furnishing interest. In a second phase, IKEA was aiming to optimize the creative execution of the 2014 catalogue by measuring and understanding the *stomach impact* of new cover ideas.

Over the past years the feeling had grown within IKEA that the qualitative evaluation of their catalogue, done through offline focus groups in different countries around the world, could potentially be done in a different, fresher and better way. This resulted in a collaboration with InSites Consulting, for a multi-country project, using Consumer Consulting Boards. The community was launched right before the 2013 catalogue was distributed, giving IKEA the opportunity to test the impact in a realistic in-home environment and leading to a much richer understanding

The @home Community

During a 3-week period, 5 online closed platforms were set up bringing together participants from five different countries around the world (the US, China, Germany, Italy and Poland). During the first week of the community the goal was to meet the reader and understand the actual and aspirational behavior of the participants. Who is the reader and what are his/her expectations towards the brand and the catalogue? To get there we conducted - amongst others - a mood board exercise in which we asked the members to map their feelings about the IKEA brand and creative tasks on the forum of the platform *(e.g. tell us your IKEA Catalogue story)*.

After the catalogue had been dropped off at the houses of the participants (in preview, 2 weeks before the real global launch), we assessed the perception, satisfaction and level of engagement the 2013 catalogue evokes.

First impressions and second thoughts on particular aspects of the catalogue were researched (structure, pictures, stories, the mobile application...) by integrating different research techniques (e.g. collage tool, ethnographic research techniques and polls). It was important to understand how the catalogue offers both inspiration and information to the reader and whether that was done to the right extent. Moreover, we wanted to get a grip on the catalogue's lifecycle. To capture the latter, participants had to fill in a diary, giving the insights department the unique benefit of understanding the usage of the IKEA Catalogue to the fullest (e.g. *who is using the catalogue, when is it used, where is it used*). By re-activating the *@home community* in a later phase, we were able to understand *the second life of the IKEA Catalogue*.

In the final week, we investigated whether the catalogue was meeting the expectations. This gave us some first clues on the impact the new catalogue had on the brand perception and shopper behavior. In other words, what impact did it have on the business: was it bringing people to the shops, raising interest and was there a positive impact on the perception of the brand among especially *lapsed* customers?

Additionally, the *@home community* was reactivated (2 months later) to assess different creative executions of the next IKEA Catalogue cover. Via implicit measurement, we were able to tap into the minds of the participants and to understand their spontaneous associations and emotions around the new cover page. By discussing the insights and results of this test, we managed to understand the stomach impact to the fullest. To maximize

insights from this research phase, a global *@home community* was opened, in which community members (the ambassadors) of the different countries helped to better understand inter-country differences.

The IKEA Catalogue in a new jacket

Based on this research program, IKEA got a better understanding of how the IKEA Catalogue is used.

The research results led to significant changes to the app. And we now know that the new concept of the catalogue was a big step into a new and correct direction; improvements will be made to the 2014 version, based on the research results.

···

Presented at the ESOMAR 3D Congress 2013 in Boston (US).

117

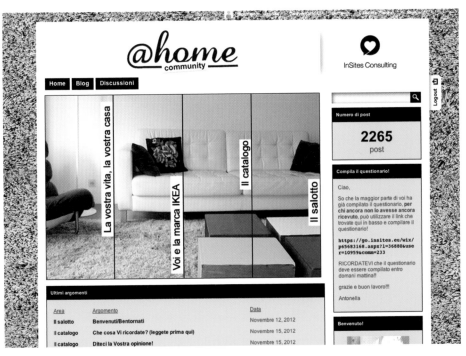

The IKEA @home comunity

DEVELOPING GO-TO-MARKET STRATEGIES FOR VODAFONE INTERNET SERVICES

To ensure that the **Vodafone** new mobile Internet services continually meet and surpass consumer expectations, a global user trial program has been established. By setting up dedicated Consumer Consulting Boards for the different services in key markets, user experiences are captured near the moment of truth. The program supports the developments of the apps and the go-to-market strategy.

Engaging first-time smartphone users

In order to grow their market share and average revenue per user (ARPU), Vodafone needed to engage with first-time smartphone users. The business objective for Vodafone in fiscal year 2012 was to launch 10 new Commercial Services and gain buy-in for up to 21 local markets. To meet and surpass the expectations of their customers, user participation in the lean development of these services was crucial. Traditional ways of testing digital services - such as user diaries, applied in *User Experience Development* - did not provide the instantaneous feedback nor the quantitative heft to convince internal stakeholders. In addition, Vodafone was looking for an integrated approach to be rolled out in multiple countries, providing a holistic view and incorporating three core areas:

- *Technical performance:* How does the service work in comparison to user expectations? Feedback on consistency and reliability guide further product development and refinement.
- *User experience:* What is the emotional resonance of the service? Does it look and feel right? Is it easy to understand?
- *Relevance:* What are the needs the service is anticipating? How to take on the positioning and messaging?

Vodafone global user trial program

The program had to support the development of the new mobile applications and define the messaging for the different markets. As some of these services were already available in the market whereas many others were in early development stage, we needed an approach that could gather actionable insights to fine-tune and understand the usage of existing apps, but also more fundamental technical feedback and user experience for the earlier versions of new apps. To allow Vodafone customers to take on the role of consultant in the launch of these services, the selection of the participant group was crucial. To get the richest information from the discussions, we did not only invite the target group of first-time smartphone users who could collaborate on the applications based on their own expectations. We also involved a group of more experienced smartphone users who are highly involved and can push the expectations.

A dedicated sub-community of 75 participants was set up for every service to be tested, in different 3-week waves and involving multiple key markets (Portugal, Spain, Italy, Germany, the Netherlands and the UK) in their native language. By enlarging the user base wave after wave, the communities were evolving towards a more structural Consumer Consulting Board. This hybrid approach, combining blogs and discussions with live chat conversations (for detailed Q&A sessions with the developer team) and short surveys (to get a pre- and post-impression on satisfaction and recommendation) allowed for swift reactivations of the communities whenever necessary.

Follow the customer journey

Together with Vodafone we developed a framework for their innovation process in which the Consumer Consulting Board is vital for testing future services. By mapping the entire customer journey and highlighting triggers and barriers. Vodafone customers take on a central role in the development of new digital services. So far, the screening and prioritization analysis led to the launch of *Guardian, Protect, Cloud, Contacts, Discover* and *joyn*. The research also supported the go-to-market strategy including volume uptake forecasts in each country.

••

Presented at the 2013 Merlien Qualitative 360 event in Berlin (DE).

TWEETAWAYS

Organizations should reserve a seat
on their board for the *Chief Consumer
Officer*, representing consumers on the
highest hierarchical level
@kristofdewulf

We need to make consumers an integral
part of everything we do: we need to
stop talking and start listening.
@MK0903

Insights generated through research
communities have proven to be 82%
more effective in the market
@annaliezze

In a compilation of 1,193 commercially successful innovations by Eric von
Hippel (MIT), 60% came from consumers
@thomastroch

The power of everyday people is driving
monumental change
@PGCMO

4

Making global brands locally relevant

From Global to Universal Brands

by Tom De Ruyck & Anneleen Boullart

Say *Hello* to a brave new world

We are witnessing a true gravitational shift in how our global society is organized and lives. One may even speak of a true tipping point when looking at the following striking facts and figures:

- By 2020 the collective GDP of the **emerging markets** will overtake that of the developed economies for the very first time. Already today multinational companies like **P&G** and **Unilever** are generating more than half of their revenues from these *new* economies.[1] Unilever wants to double its turnover in the next 5 years, and the majority of that growth needs to come from emerging markets.
- For the first time in the history of mankind more than half of the world's population is living in cities.[2] **Urbanization** seems to be one of the main recipes behind the success of the booming markets.
- Finally, the **world's population has never been younger:** more than a third is younger than 30 years old, in some emerging markets this is even half of the population.[3] An emerging young urban middle class is the engine behind the world's fastest growing economies.

These are numbers that speak. The Asian countries are writing a big part of this new story. According to Bloomberg, 5 of the top 10 emerging economies lie in Asia.[4] China, Indonesia and India are leading the pack. Other growth regions are Latin America (with Brazil as the new giant) and Central & Eastern Europe (with growing markets Russia, Poland and Turkey). South-Africa is an example for the whole Southern part of Africa, where the term used for the new emerging middle class - Black Diamonds - is illustrative for the potential that is breaking through.

It is the rising middle class in all of these regions that is the foundation for significant business potential. The OECD (part of the United Nations) expects that the middle classes in China and India alone will grow from 6% of the total global middle class today to 41% by 2030.[5] No need to say that, given the saturation of economic growth in Western-Europe and North-America, future growth for companies is to grasp in these new economies. In the *old* markets nonetheless the battle to protect what has been built over the years has started as well.

Global brands seem to be in pole position to get to this future first. In a world populated by young urban citizens who are increasingly connected with the world-wide-web, global brands are the ones who can probably leverage the most on their global appeal and potential scale of their strong brands. A perfect illustration of the fact that we live in a globalized and connected world is the influence online video site **YouTube**

Making global brands locally relevant

had on music preferences of people around the globe. Two major things happened since YouTube gained popularity as a music streaming channel. On the one hand a globalization of the hit lists. All of a sudden, a South-Korean guy scores a global monster hit out of nowhere. On the other hand the *long tail* of music taste is killed to some extent. We could state that YouTube has created a more global and uniform music taste. The question is: *are big global brands as powerful as YouTube is for our taste in music?* With the majority of the ▢ world's online population being connected with brands in one way or another,[6] it seems as if strong (global) brands have everything in place to create global tribes of fans. But is this the whole story or just one side of the same coin?

Making global brands locally relevant

It is probably too easy to say that global brands with their global appeal and scale have an easy job in conquering the world. Worldwide we notice a not to neglect anti-trend of globalization: going hyperlocal. **Noma** in Copenhagen, the best restaurant in the world, is an example of this anti-trend. At Noma, only local or home-grown products are used. The chef prefers to work with ingredients authentically produced by craftsmen

Restaurant Noma in Copenhagen

and with a certain level of pride for the local heritage. Signs like this indicate that although we live in a globalized world, it is still important to be rooted locally.

The same goes for brands: they need to be locally relevant and if needed adapt their product offering and the way brand and product activation are executed to the local reality. If they do not do this, they will fail. An interesting example of a global brand which experienced this is **McDonald's** in India.[7] McDonald's only became successful in that huge market after making two adaptations to their product portfolio: offering a vegetarian option and making the food slightly spicier. But it was not enough to only adapt the product. They also discovered that Indians want to see how the food is prepared: separate open kitchens are now used to prepare vegetables and meat products. The real local breakthrough came when McDonald's lowered the entry price point by introducing special menus and when they started positioning themselves as the family restaurant to have joyful moments together. This case shows that it is not about slightly tweaking your brand and products; it is about rethinking and localizing all aspects of the marketing mix. Different markets have different cultural codes, preferences in taste and retail systems that all need to be taken into account. All of them will have a major influence on defining the product portfolio and on creating successful strategies for local brand and product activation.

Global or local, or combining both? In interviews we conducted with 21 senior executives from international/global brands (amongst others: **Heineken**, **Durex**, **Esprit**, **Eastpak**, **H.J. Heinz**, **eBay**, **BBC**, **MasterCard** and **PepsiCo**), all of them were touching upon this paradox. On the one hand, brands need to go global and grasp the new opportunities that are out there. In order to achieve this one needs global appeal and global scale. On the other hand, you will never be successful if you do not succeed in becoming locally relevant and if you do not start building local best practices.

Made (t)here, for (t)here

Local competition is strong, fast & different

In almost every industry and product category local alternatives for global brands are created. And it goes even further. Local companies are creating products for a whole region. **Lenovo** is a Chinese producer of smartphones who is now conquering the huge markets in India and Indonesia with their low-cost smartphones strategy. And the new economic giants have the ambition to export unique high-quality goods to Western markets as well. Already today, Brazilian fashion designers proudly celebrate the heritage of their nation on the catwalks of the fashion capitals of the world. Local competition is hard, but also different. For some aspects, the emerging markets take a different route than their developed counterparts: they are *leapfrogging*. Regarding Internet technology for example, the PC phase was skipped and they jumped immediately onto the mobile web. That is only one of the reasons why one needs to take an eye on a country like Brazil when it comes to expertise in successfully advertising on social networks and knowledge in the space of mobile marketing. Another way in which best practices are transferred between countries is the practice of *reverse innovation*. Strategies applied in or products created for emerging economies come back to the developed world. In Southern Europe - a region suffering from the global economic crisis - some laundry brands use strategies they applied with success in emerging markets like India to make their high-quality brand affordable for the lower middle class: smaller packs with powder or liquid for one week of laundry.

Finally, the way in which and speed by which most companies in these markets are innovating is different as well: *innovation through commercialization* is the norm. Asian companies do not spend months or even years on testing and fine-tuning new products in labs based on big piles of research. A good enough product is immediately thrown onto the market and based on the feedback from the first consumers the product is fine-tuned in a process of mostly 4 iterative loops.

It is clear that companies need to merge global with local and adapt to the local business reality. Be brave in this new world and grasp the new opportunities, as there is a lot to gain... and to learn.

Creating a Universal Brand

To indicate the importance of merging global with local on different levels, it is better to speak of a universal brand than of a global brand. After all, global appeal is about being able to build your brand globally based on a universal insight. An insight that evokes the same *Aha, it's me* feeling among people from different cultures around the globe. A strong insight is equal to a sort of *Aha* experience: a combination of surprise and something familiar. It entails a view on something which was implicit all that time. The second basic aspect of a strong consumer insight is relevance. A strong insight automatically calls for familiarity *(It's me)*, sometimes even to the extent that you may even learn things about yourself that you were not aware of before. Next to that, a brand(ed) universe needs to be created around that (cluster of) insight(s). The brand's universe needs to be wide enough to allow for localizations on the brand, product & activation level. Thirdly, the leadership behind the brand needs to understand how to make the local teams enthusiastic about the global strategy. The global brand leadership team also needs to stimulate the sharing of best practices between countries with likewise challenges. Lastly, local brand team members who have gained specific knowledge about a particular domain

O GIGANTE NÃO ESTÁ MAIS ADORMECIDO.

'KEEP WALKING, BRAZIL

JOHNNIE WALKER

The 'Keep walking, Brazil' campaign

(because of the specific situation in their market) need to be put in the global driver seat to lead that specific capability.

A brand which does this well is *Johnnie Walker*. Their tagline ☐ *Keep on walking* is based on a universal insight that fits well with their product and the category they are in: being ambitious in life and never giving up.[8] They created a brand universe that stays true to this starting point, but that is strong enough to be adapted locally. In Brazil for example the tagline was tweaked to: *Keep on walking, Brazil*. Smart move, as it is touching upon the rise of Brazil as a new super power, combined with the strong we-feeling and the national pride which is typical for Brazilians. Brazil is a huge and very diverse country, also in terms of attitudes and ambition levels of the population. Therefore, it is great to observe that Johnnie Walker used different activation campaigns in the major cities of São Paulo and Rio de Janeiro. The people in the first city are more focused on personal and professional ambition, while the citizens of the latter are generally more family-oriented. The activation campaigns were taking these differences between both cities into account. Another important element in the campaign's success was the use of social media and mobile marketing. Brazil is one of the leading countries in both domains, given the high level of adoption of mobile Internet in the country. This was leading to best practices that were useful for local teams in other countries as well.

129

Companies behind universal brands need to be *open* and *agile*. First of all, having an active dialogue with consumers around the world is crucial to understand different cultures, to follow their evolutions and to grasp the new reality. And in order to get to the future first, agile and diverse brand teams are a must these days. Ideally, a team is a mix of global strategists and local brand builders who constantly collaborate. They react quickly to new developments and base their plan of attack on the global strategy in combination with strong local insights and regional best practices.

Getting under the skin of a different culture

It remains important to have a global helicopter view, but gaining local knowledge and relevance will ultimately determine whether you will really be successful in local markets. This is beautifully summarized in a quote by **Nelson Mandela**.

....

'If you speak A language a man understands, you speak to his MIND. If you speak HIS language, you speak to his HEART'

Nelson Mandela

....

How do you get under the skin of the population of a country with its cultural codes and preferences? By taking the time to observe and interact with a diverse group of local people:

- **Observe consumers and start the dialogue:** if you really want to get to know a target group and its culture, facts and figures are not enough to get a holistic view. It is important to observe local consumers and to have a

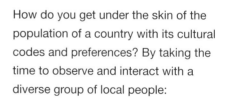

dialogue with them. Only by being connected, one can develop a thorough understanding of what is going on.

- **Be connected with a diverse group of people:** it is vital to be connected with a diverse group of participants who reflect the diversity of the target group or country one is dealing with. Emerging economies are characterized by a wide variety of social classes, life styles and even cultural differences within the country. The latter is definitely the case in large countries like China, Russia and Brazil.

- **Take your time:** it takes time to understand new target groups, cultures and realities. By taking time with a larger group of participants whom you get

to know from different angles, you will truly get under their skin.

- **Be agile:** today's business reality asks for fast action and reaction. Especially in the new Asian economies launching new products and adapting existing ones goes at the speed of light. Therefore, it is important to work with a research method that allows you to take better decisions faster.

If we bring all these needs together, we end up with a Consumer Consulting Board: a larger group of people brought together on an online closed community platform, to structurally collaborate with each other over a longer period of time. A group of key consumers who help you shape your business.

Walking our own talk

In the second chapter of this book, we outlined our approach for establishing, managing and analyzing the output of research communities. The fundamentals of this approach work on a global scale. But, just like the brands we are working for, we need to localize our way of working from country to country. Research-on-research taught us that adapting elements of the following dimensions is crucial in order to establish a healthy Consumer Consulting Board:

- **Language:** out of meta-research on our communities we know that members participate best if they can write in their own language. Taking part in an English-speaking community for a non-native speaker can be hard. It has a rather negative influence on the intensity of participation and the level of detail and nuance when one is writing. That is why our default option is to conduct communities in the native language of the participant. For a global project to evaluate the **IKEA** Catalogue for example, we conducted local communities in the US, China, Germany, Italy and Poland. That being said, there can be good reasons to opt for a multi-national English-speaking community: non-native executives of the company who want to follow the discussion, limited budgets

or the fact that one is in search for global consensus on a given subject rather than an understanding of local differences. An example of the latter is our global *Shape-It* Consumer Consulting Board for ketchup giant **H.J. Heinz**. The goal of this project was to come to a new and uniform design for the shape of the next-generation ketchup bottle. Participants from more than 10 countries took part in the same community to reach global consensus.

- **Moderator:** the *Cultural Iceberg* model of the American anthropologist **Edward Hall** suggests that language is only a small part of culture.[9] In order to grasp the local context and situation fully, our preference is to work with a moderator who does not only speak the language, but also understands all the other cultural aspects of a country (common values, beliefs, traditions, attitudes and perceptions), next to the local market situation and the business context.

In order to fully understand to what extent localization of our methodology is needed, we conducted several studies with moderators from our *Global Community Moderator Network* (active in 30 different countries) and with local research participants. This way we co-created best practices for the different markets we are operating in. We found that it is important to adapt your community to the local culture on 5 aspects.

The directions in which the adaptations are made can be explained by the work of the Dutch academic researcher **Geert Hofstede** and his 5 dimensions to explain cultural differences between countries.[10] For each of the 30 countries we do research in, we have developed a full overview of best practices for every single aspect of community management. Below we explain the different dimensions in more detail and illustrate them with some striking examples.

1. **Reason to participate:** from the first invitation e-mail to join the community and onwards, it needs to be clear what is in it for the participants. In almost all countries, the main reason to participate is the possibility to have an influence on the future of a brand or a product.

   Next to this, we noticed that some countries are more extrinsically motivated than others. This is especially the case in the USA and Eastern European countries, but for different reasons. Americans consider it to be normal that there is a payment in return for performance. In most Eastern European countries on the other hand a (monetary) incentive is perceived as a nice extra on top of their monthly income. Furthermore, in Eastern Europe, it is a must to gain the trust of the members. Trust in the fact that the agency or company behind the community will not harm them in any way. And trust in the fact that they will really get their incentive. The preferred type of incentive differs from country to country. It is an illusion to think that **PayPal** fits all.

   In Asian countries such as India and China, intrinsic motivation is important: they like to be connected with aspirational brands and share their wisdom. In Latin-American countries like Brazil, the social aspect has a higher importance in the overall mix of reasons to become a Board member.

2. **Technology:** mobile technology is developing rapidly and adoption of mobile Internet is increasing worldwide. It is a valuable medium to get access to another type of data: more *personal* and *contextual* information. But given the situation in some markets, where most consumers only have access to the web through their mobile phones,

Language is only 10% of Culture

133

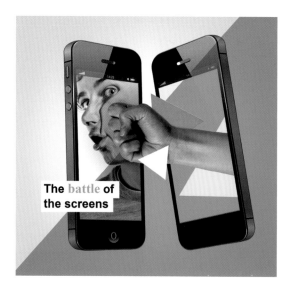

The battle of the screens

we need to change our preferred medium to reach out to them. As mobile-only users are the new reality, it is a necessity to adapt our way of asking questions or giving tasks. In the scenario of mobile-only communities, one needs to work more task-based and ask more questions that can be answered in a short and convenient way. Wisely rethinking the mix of research tools and adapting them to the small screen is a final must do.

3. **Conversation guide:** a different culture also means different attitudes and values, leading to a different way of reacting to certain questions, tasks and exercises moderators want participants to perform. Some cultures for instance love to share a lot of details about themselves and their lives. Others prefer to talk about the group, which is consid-

ered to be a safer option. This could be seen as a projective technique to let people talk about their own situation, free of any pressure. The same holds for co-creation exercises. It is not a given in every culture that people are used to taking initiative. They feel better when they are only asked to give feedback about what already exists. It is important to map the country that one is working in on those two axes (*me* versus *we* and *feedback* versus *co-creation*) and to adapt the way of writing and (re) mixing topics for the conversation guide to it.

4. **Role of the moderator:** one does not only need to adapt the way of inviting and incentivizing the members, the medium of data collection and the nature of the topics in the conversation guide. The role of the moderator is also perceived differently from one country to the other. In Brazil a moderator needs to facilitate and start the discussion. His/her role lies more in the background. But it is also expected from the moderator that he/she is steering the discussion in the right direction when it is going off topic. In Russia on the other hand, the moderator needs to be strict and almost literally direct the members to the next question or task they need to look into. The moderator in Brazil is more a social peer; he/she needs to be a formal professional in China and a like-minded person to exchange

wisdom with in India. It is crucial to know and manage all these different expectations when running (multi-country or global) Consumer Consulting Boards.

5. **Gamification:** adding elements of gamification to the community brings more richness to the table. In our research-on-research among our moderators we learned that the level of and the intensity by which you gamify your Consumer Consulting Board needs to differ between countries. In Spain for example they absolutely love the gamification elements, even to the extent that the local moderator includes additional game aspects in the topics and the newsletters. On the contrary, in Germany it is wise to limit it to a minimal level as it is culturally less accepted.

The above elements show that in multi-country projects you need to start from a master conversation guide. But adaptations both in content and style of the topics and the way of moderating will be key elements in making the community a real success. Experience taught us that, when analyzing the comments in the community, it is as important to pay equal attention to how people say things as to what they say. There is a lot of symbolism and cultural meaning in the words and metaphors used by participants to express themselves. Understanding these can be of great value to fully grasp the cultural differ-

ences around certain issues. Last but not least, it is important to walk our own talk and invite community members to become a part of the research process in order to fill our blind spots.[11] They can even become our eyes and ears into the world around them. They can observe and share information about groups in society who until now have been less capable of taking part in research communities, adding again a totally different dimension to what we already know.

From global discoveries to local impact

How to develop a *universal insight*? It all starts with immersing into the local culture and getting close to the local consumer. One first needs to understand the cultural context. Next up is gaining insights about the people in the target group and understanding the product category you are operating in: Creating a holistic view on the lives, dreams and fears of your consumers and how they perceive and value the category in general and your competitors in specific. In the final stage of the process one tries to define how the brand itself is perceived and what it means to people. By combining and connecting the different insights we craft, we can define a cluster of insights that have potentially

Gaining local relevance

global appeal: universal insights.

In our international/global projects, native moderators run the local communities and a global project team is connecting the dots together with them. By consequence, we are able to combine the best insights on a global and a local level. Moreover, we ask the members of the Consumer Consulting Board to help us with detecting which insights really have global appeal. We do that by bringing together participants from the different local communities into a global English speaking discussion room. In this global room, we discuss the global appeal of a cluster of insights in a qualitative way among the ambassadors of the different local communities. In a global community project for a non-alcoholic beverages producer, we worked with local communities in 18 different countries. Near the end of the process, ambassadors from the 18 countries gathered in the global room. We tested 5 key insights on their global appeal. Only

2 were accepted by the majority of the crowd, illustrating the value of this stage in which we go back to the participants.

The global brand leadership team needs to make sure that all local teams are behind the universal insight. It is important to create internal enthusiasm and understanding about it. In a second stage, the local teams need to get the full details of the nuances in their market. The output from their local arm of the Consumer Consulting Board is a treasure of information about their target group, the local competition within the category and the local perceptions of the brand. This will help them to see what products need to be included in the product range and if adaptations to the local taste are required. For **PepsiCo** Turkey a local *Ruffles* community helped the local brand and marketing team to give brand and product activation campaigns local relevance, while staying true to the global strategy.

Stay hungry for opportunities and new knowledge

In today's globalized world it is important to stay connected with the fast developments that are going on and to learn and react quickly. People living in the so-called developed world need to find inspiration in what is happening in emerging markets to grasp the tremendous opportunities in those new markets and to gain new knowledge and develop tactics for counter-balancing the status quo in the West.

This article outlined how important it is to understand cultural differences and local market situations. Members of your local Consumer Consulting Board will help you to gain that understanding. They will help you get to a strong universal insight driving global brand leadership and will bring you the agility and localization needed to connect in the most powerful way with consumers all over the globe.

Ready to discover some new territory?

Sharing is Caring

How to build a
Gen Y proof
global brand?

by Joeri Van den Bergh

One in three global citizens is part of Generation Y, aka the Millennials. In many emerging markets the sheer size of this new consumer generation is even over 50 per cent. With many *baby boomers* retiring and some of them already passing away, future proof global brands urgently need to adapt to the Gen Y's consumer needs.

The AND/AND generation

In my book *How Cool Brands Stay Hot*,[12] I refer to Generation Y, aka the Millennials (born in the 1980s and in the first half of the 90s), as the ultimate products of our postmodern society. They are both individualistic and very sociable. They have traditional family values but are very tolerant and open. They have a strong work ethic but want a balanced life and lots of leisure time as well. They do not want to make the same mistakes as their baby boomer parents who traded in a fair amount of their spare time to succeed in life. They want to get rich and believe they will earn a lot, but at the same time they value enriching experiences even more. They cherish their local roots and love brands with local anchors but also think very globally, in career as well as in friendships and travel. Generation Y is a far more positive generation than Generation X, with a stronger belief in a better future and a better world. They are more engaged, strongly voice their opinions and act upon their ideas. They feel empowered to change the world themselves (just think of the *Arab Spring*, *Occupy Wall Street* or the UK student protests) and claim the authorship of their own lives in every single aspect. Gen Y's social usage of technology is one of the big differences with other generations. On the other hand it is technology that is unifying them globally. It connects them to infinite knowledge, friends and entertainment. All of this clearly affects the way marketing, branding and research targeting this new consumer group should evolve. GenYers will only stay interested in your brand if it succeeds in wetting their curiosity. Keeping your brand cool by incremental innovations is the key to winning their loyalty. Gen Y wants it right here, right now. Their need for instant gratification must be satisfied by immediate advantages. At the same time constantly renewing your brands and products whilst staying real and true to your own brand DNA and unique identity are essential.

How Cool Brands Stay Hot: Branding to Generation Y

Making global brands locally relevant

Marketing and branding WITH Millennials

GenYers are more marketing-savvy and will immediately see through fake marketing strategies. Honesty and transparency are important aspects of successful and future-proof brands. Again, both the uniqueness and honesty GenYers look for in brands are nothing more than a reflection of the times they were raised in. They were born in a society that celebrated individual success and were stimulated to become unique and special. Gen Y appreciates directness and closeness. Instead of making distant image claims in advertising, brands should demonstrate what they stand for by their (locally relevant) deeds. For *Generation X*, brands were communicating status and had to express that they were winners.

For Generation Y, brands are tools and creative platforms for communicating who they are. Brands and products are seen by this generation as important in creating their own personal and unique narrative. They provide them with a way to stand out from the mass and stimulate discerning usage. At the same time, successful brands have to bring social acceptance for youngsters in their reference groups. A brand will only be relevant if Gen Y can participate, co-create and co-shape the brand identity

whilst receiving the most important currency to them: content for offline as well as online conversations. *I am what I create* is a strong belief among this new consumer generation. After sharing text, pictures, video and audio found online through social networks, they are now more interested in creating something themselves, because it is per definition more unique and more shareable. It is comparable to baking your own cake rather than to buy one and then sharing it with your friends or colleagues. Creativity became a status symbol. Creative entrepreneurs are the new superstars, whether it is in gastronomy, design, fashion, app development or any other business. Young people like to associate with people, brands and visual formats with a creative image. That is why Facebook trends such as *owling*, *planking*, *leisure diving*, *tilting* and the *Harlem Shake* went viral globally. They are easy-to-copy formats that still give young people the idea that they belong to a creative group of people. It is also the reason why an easy-to-use photo App like *Instagram* is so successful. It turns every smartphone snapshot into a work of art and you can immediately share it with your friends and instantly enjoy the received *likes* and comments. Companies, brands and products that not only connect young people with each other but also facilitate and endorse creativity will be the winners of the next years. GenYers like the idea of being in full control of everything and don't passively accept what is given to them. They embrace ownership of

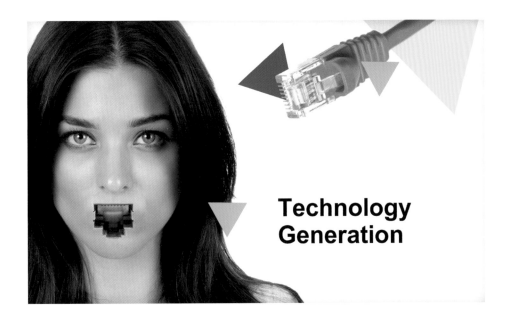

Technology Generation

content and want to be able to edit and change their environment every minute. Marketers should adopt the same open source philosophy. A brand is not what a company wants it to be, it is what Gen Y consumers want it to be. The real job of marketers today is to give the brand back to its fans and consumers.

Global citizens rooted in local communities

Gen Y is certainly the most globally connected generation ever. Internet, social media, *Skype*, *FaceTime*, instant and text messaging, cheap airline tickets, couch surfing… They have all the tools and opportunities to explore the

world and be in touch with a diversity of cultural influences. Many of them will spend at least one or two years studying or working abroad. They see the world as a global village without borders. On the other hand, we know from our research that Millennials care most about their immediate social circle.[13] Their friends and family are key and they tend to largely identify with their own village or city and with their own country. That national feeling of pride and the need to be in touch with the local community should not be underestimated. As **Tom De Ruyck** wrote in his article on universal brands in this book: *'Successful global brands understand that they need to have a local relevance and connection'*. *'The needs of Gen Y in Turkey are fundamentally different from those in Sweden, Mexico or India'*, says **Peter Jung**, Senior Business Leader at **MasterCard International**. *'So it forces us to tailor our products and services to*

the region we're addressing. Turkey is an enormous Gen Y market, 60% of the population is under 30. What they need is a safe way to buy things online so we've developed a product that addresses this need. In some BRIC markets shops don't accept cards, so instead of swiping or entering a PIN, we are delivering ways to pay with a smartphone since the penetration of mobile devices is much higher than the penetration of card devices. In Mexico for instance social status is a major driver of behavior - Gen Y in Mexico sees value in being able to access fashion brands or experience something that their peers may not.' Peter Jung calls this *social credibility*. **Francisco Bethencourt**, Senior Director Strategy & Marketing at **PepsiCo**, agrees. *'Brand execution and activation, and ultimately sales, are always done in local communities'*, **he says in an interview with us.** *'So you need to be relevant and authentic in that local setting and be aware of local issues that are important to your consumers. It is a balance between keeping brand strategy and positioning but allowing flexibility in lo-*

cal execution to develop authentic and relevant solutions to your consumers locally. A common building platform in your communication and brand strategy to prevent fragmentation of your positioning is required but you also have to activate through different cultural cues to stay relevant with a particular audience or community. Location-based and mobile marketing allow to interact with your consumer depending on where he is, like a sport's venue, or movie theatre or shopping center so that you can customize promotional activities and introductions to new products. Big companies such as **McDonald's** *and* **Coca-Cola** *create a global emotional connection with the brand through their campaigns but they understand that the local activation is key to connect with Millennials today. If you look at music festivals or independent film festivals, the local flavors became much more important. So hyperlocalization is a trend in society and brands need to understand that and come up with new ideas that cater for that new trend.'*

Conclusion

Generation Y, or the Millennials, the children of the large baby boomer generation, is a much bigger, more influential generation than the previous Gen X generation. Their impact on society, politics and business in the next 3 decades will soon overshadow the achievements of their parents. I'd like to end my contribution with the point that the new global consumer is no longer waiting for an invitation to co-create brands. Gen Y is collaborating and associating with like-minded people to build their own unique brands out of the components that transparent companies provide them with. As former global brand director of **Nike SB**, **Gert Kerkstoel**, states in the foreword of my book: *'The first question marketing executives should ask is: 'Who cares?' as in, 'Really, who are the people who truly care for my brand and why? And what can I do for and with them?' That is very different from launching your next idea into the world being locked up in a meeting room. Generation Y immediately knows when something is just a marketing construction.'*

The Triumph Generation

Connecting 100 urban Millennials around the world

In the summer of 2011 InSites Consulting and **MTV Networks** teamed up to create *Crushed Ice*, a global online community of 🔲 influential youth[14] discussing what they observed around them in their local cities during six consecutive weeks. We selected one hundred 18- to 29-year-olds living in 15 cities around the world. They were all screened on both their innovator-influencer profile and activity degree. Themes that were tackled included shopping and fashion, in-home entertainment, going out, food & drinks and travel. Other general evolutions and societal trends were derived from their daily observations. One of those trends was their desire for responsible global brands. We learned that being a responsible brand is also about people. Creating safe working places and offering a fair salary rather than exploiting employees or workers are synonyms to social branding. They like companies that put clear societal goals forward and act upon them without bragging. They dislike companies that actively communicate about *CSR* (Corporate Social Responsibility) programs, which is seen as *green washing*. Because eco claims became just another advertising strategy in the first decade of the 2000s, GenYers are very cautious in

really believing what a brand is telling about protecting the environment. When sports fashion brand **Puma** worked together with **Yves Behar**'s *Fuse* project to design a shoe box that would reduce the ecological footprint, many of them reacted skeptically on blogs. Puma's viral movie explained that using a bag instead of a box reduced the cardboard by 65%, eventually resulting in a lowered usage of paper (trees), energy, water and a lower carbon dioxide emissions. However youngsters called it brand propaganda, questioning the positive impact of the design, highlighting that 77% of the carbon footprint in shoes come from raw materials (leather, rubber and cotton) and only a mere 5% comes from the packaging. To win credibility with CSR programs to this generation, brands and companies should keep 3 things in mind:

Yves Behar's Clever Little Bag for PUMA

The wisdom
of crowds

1. **Gen Y will rarely deliberately choose a brand because of its charity or ecological programs.**
   A brand's socially responsible image will never make up for poor quality or other basics. Rather than communicating green aspects, they want brands to focus on how an innovation makes a product itself better and at the same time it happens to be produced in a responsible way too.

2. **What really makes a difference is when a company is advocating responsible actions to other players in the industry and becoming a change agent.**

Examples are: **Cadbury** for using fair trade in all products, **Mars** committing to become exploitation-free by 2020 through **Rainforest alliance** & UTZ certification, **Bodyshop** (for its values), **Sainsbury's** (fair trade), and **Johnson & Johnson** (minimizing environmental impact).

3. **Gen Y does not like to be marketed TO but like to do marketing WITH:**
   Instead of bombarding young people with programs, they want to make a difference themselves by owning the values and choosing themselves how and where charitable contributions will go.

Our **Global** Community Moderator Network

by Liesbeth Dambre & Els Cocquyt

Our feet on the ground in over 30 countries

Market challenges

Today the market research industry is facing two important challenges. First, a lot of new research methodologies are entering the market and according to the latest ⬚ *GRIT study*,[15] research communities are the rising star. Next to that, a lot of global brands are looking at emerging markets to grasp new opportunities. It is absolutely critical for clients that they understand and connect with consumers wherever these consumers may live around the world.

Global AND local

We are a global company and have been conducting Consumer Consulting Boards on a global scale for many years, bringing in a number of new challenges. We believe that you can only get rich insights out of your Consumer Consulting Boards if they are moderated by experienced local moderators who can communicate with participants in their mother tongue, who understand their culture, their brand preferences and the current challenges in their country. That is why we created a *Global Community Moderator Network*, consisting of experienced local moderators, consulting our clients

on a global scale, by applying their local knowledge and experience.

Open collaboration

As *openness* is one of InSites Consulting's key values, we believe that open collaboration is the future for us as well. We are building strong global capabilities by tapping into the experience of the best people across the globe. They have the local knowledge, so we do not only count on them for moderation, but also for localizing our moderation approach for each country, as already stated by **Tom De Ruyck** in the beginning of this chapter. Combining the advantages of being global - which means having one global methodology, one global vision and one global project team - with those of tapping into the local moderator's knowledge of culture and market, allows us to service our clients globally, making their brands relevant on a local scale.

Managing the network

Our network grows via the many contacts we developed throughout years of experience in running international qualitative research projects. As you can see on the map, at this moment we have InSites Consulting certified moderators available in over 30 countries across all continents. This includes emerging markets such as BRICMIST, Europe & United Arab Emirates.

Overview of our Global Community Moderator Network

As the network is becoming larger and larger we have invested a lot in professionalizing the network management. We have introduced several tools and procedures managing our network in an effective and efficient way.

Our network management consists of an internal management system which includes recruitment and selection procedures, a centralized information tool, an evaluation system and contract handling. This system allows us to gear up rapidly when setting up new projects and partnerships in new countries.

A second aspect of efficient network management is the launch of an e-learning platform which allows our moderators to learn about our philosophy, tools, processes and moderation guidelines at their own pace. This platform contains e-trainings but also a number of tests and homework tasks to perform before becoming a certified member of our network. Of course this is always combined with a live Q&A session with their coach at InSites Consulting after the training.

Co-creation

But receiving a certification is not the end; it is only the start of a continuous relationship. Our certified network members have access to the *Moderator Square*, a community platform built for InSites Consulting certified moderators only. On this platform, moderators can stay up-to-date on the latest online moderator techniques and have unique access to the InSites Consulting know-how. But this is not a one-way communication channel; this platform is a real research community which we will use to do research-about-research, together with our moderators. So we will not only bring their knowledge of the local culture and market into our client projects, we will also co-create the future of Consumer Consulting Boards with them.

148

CERTIFIED MEMBER
COMMUNITY MODERATOR NETWORK

'I'm always very excited when a new international InSites Consulting project is about to start because you get to meet and work with other fellow moderators from all over the world and share experiences with them. You get to witness the essential universal human beliefs and attitudes but also the peculiarities and unique viewpoints of each individual country locally. And all of this takes place in a vibrant and exciting yet relaxed atmosphere provided by the InSites Consulting team. The InSites Consulting project manager is the director orchestrating a symphony of enthusiastic and well experienced moderators, offering direction, motivation, support and the desire to strive for excellence.'
Silvia Iranzo Ferrandis (Spain)

'It's really fascinating to work on a project where you get to see cross-cultural differences as they emerge in real time. It's a dynamic collaboration which can be more enjoyable than flying out to observe groups abroad and being stuck in the dark, eating crisps behind a one-way mirror!'
Tom Woodnutt (UK)

'I enjoy getting to know and working together with moderators abroad and exchange experiences. I even could brush up my Spanish a bit with the Mexican colleague during the last project :-) InSites Consulting is always open to your suggestions and recommendations as they regard YOU as the expert for YOUR country. To sum it up: as a moderator for InSites Consulting I really have the feeling of taking market research to the next step into the future - and this feels very exciting and satisfying.'
Jens Krämer (Germany)

'A privilege to be a part of the moderator network, working with a great community of participants and the InSites Consulting team in an innovative, thought-provoking and creative way to really generate great insights for clients. It continues to satisfy my interest in human nature and behavior as the energy and enthusiasm from the participants fully engaged on a project and with each other is great to be a part of.'
Marie Walters (UK)

'I enjoyed being in contact with the moderators of other countries, during the debrief you can have cultural differences, you can focus on an axis which you had not thought of, in short it allows to improve yourself.'
Patricia Facchin (France)

149

In the past 18 months the InSites Consulting *ForwaR&D Lab* team traveled around the world to spread the word about Consumer Consulting Boards. Some highlights out of **more than 150 talks:**

We are proud to be the hosts of the workshops on *research communities* of **ESOMAR, MRS, MOA, BAQMaR, SAMRA, AMA** and **SMRD**; giving us the unique opportunity to share our expertise with researchers around the world.

Making global brands locally relevant

TWEETAWAYS

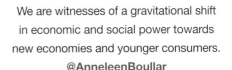

We are witnesses of a gravitational shift in economic and social power towards new economies and younger consumers.
@AnneleenBoullar

By 2020 the collective GDP of emerging markets will overtake those of developed economies for the first time.
@tomderuyck

If you speak a language a man understands, you speak to his mind. If you speak his language, you speak to his heart.
@NelsonMandela

153

Gen Y wants it right here, right now. Satisfy their need for instant gratification with incremental innovations to your brand.
@Joeri_InSites

A brand is not what you want it to be, but what consumers want it to be: marketing's real job is to give the brand back to its fans.
@Joeri_InSites

5

Shaping
the future
together

The **bright future**
of Consumer
Consulting Boards

by Annelies Verhaeghe & Tom De Ruyck

Communities are the rising star within market research. Whereas initially many companies started off with a pilot project, more and more brands are now going for structural collaboration with their consumers. Research communities are more than just a trend. They are here to stay and will continue to gain ground. At the same time, they will always be in a state of *perpetual beta*. The context in which consumers live is changing drastically. It is affecting their behavior accordingly. Hence, we need to keep on reinventing ourselves. So what is next for research communities?

Catch me if you can

Consumers' online and offline lives are blending, they use different multi-media interchangeably, are always on-the-go and create their very own cocktail of attitudes. They have to spread their attention across multiple touchpoints that fight for their attention, making them more difficult to grasp!

In the future, communities will be conducted where the consumer leads us. Smartphones are our new buddies. Whereas today computers are - in most countries - still the dominant device to take part in our communities, we will evolve to *mobile-only* Consumer Consulting Boards. Going mobile will also give us access to new information: through geo-location, we will be able to

link a conversation to a location. That way, new and additional data will be available to contextualize our findings. Consumers will be able to voice their opinion orally which will directly be transcribed in a textual format on the community. Through video, we will be able to grasp the offline consumer reality. Most importantly, mobile communities will create a direct consumer line that is available 24/7 in the true sense of the word. This real-time feedback will empower companies with a Board to react in a more agile way than ever before.

Mobility will go further than just one device. We will blend our community with other social media which are a more natural touchpoint for consumers. We recently conducted a community in *The Voice of Holland* for **RTL & Talpa** where we embedded our community in the Facebook page of the program. The research community of the future will allow participants to access the community via the platform of their choice. This means that there will no longer be only one community platform. The term *community* will increasingly refer to a group of engaged consumers who have a common goal to help a brand, but they can be spread across many platforms. We will also approach recruitment of community members from this perspective: online access panels will be abandoned in favor of approaching consumers in places where they spontaneously gather. We will fish the river in which the fish are swimming. The panel providers of the future will most likely be Facebook, Twitter and other influential social media. Also on the client side, we will need to get more creative in order to grasp their attention. There is now abundance of data. The more structural the collaboration with consumers becomes, the more data will be collected. The challenge for the future will be to turn the ever growing amount and variety of data into insights in a faster pace. This need for speed will also lead to more *fusion research*: through micro surveys - short surveys containing only a couple of questions, embedded in a community - we will be able to summarize the community members' opinions in statistics. Although not representative, this will be used increasingly for decision making. The researcher of the future will need to be an expert in creative cutting. Through text analytics and new visual analysis techniques, we will reduce big data and detect patterns across topics, regions and participants over time. At the same time, it will be about selecting inspiring content that can change the hearts, mind and actions of people behind brands. More attention will be needed for information logistics to ensure that different stakeholders in the company have access to the right information, in the right format at the right time. Applying marketing techniques on our research results will become a must!

We think less than we think we think

Consumers are bad witnesses of their own behavior. They have a hard time expressing their feelings. They say different things than they do. Recent evidence from neuropsychology teaches us that our brain has two parts:[1] a reflective and rational route, also called *system 1* which is activated when we are really thinking and an automatic and intuitive route referred to as *system 2* which makes very quick effortless decisions based on past behavior and the emotional evaluation of past actions. In more than 80% of consumer decisions, it is the more intuitive emotional system that takes the lead.

For far too long, we have engaged consumers in a too rational way. We ask them to answer questions or to consciously reflect about topics. The next wave of communities will complement this with new techniques that tap into system 2 thinking. Thanks to evolutions in neuromarketing, we are able to look into the brain of consumers. Through reaction time measurement, we can also measure the implicit attitudes of consumers. For **IKEA**, we measured the community participants' implicit emotional reactions towards the new catalogue. Based on the results, we discovered that one specific communication evoked a certain emotion. Together with the community members we were

able to reflect on this result. Also online facial recognition, galvanic skin reaction and new advances in eye tracking allow us to even capture behavioral reactions on marketing stimuli shown in the community or conversations. We will go beyond the power of the written word and evolve to more behavioral communities. Imagine for example the consequences for research if consumers' smartphones touchscreen and vibration capabilities could mimic the physical sensation of touching something. No more need to rely on purely audio-visual representations and textual descriptions. Consumer connection will happen through all the senses.

Consumer journalists

Today's consumers voice their opinions even when not being asked for it. They can make or break a brand on a scale never seen before. We see an increasing trend towards *life caching* where consumers share their lives on social media. The empowered consumers choose their own tools and moments to do so. In lots of cases they express themselves outside the Consumer Consulting Board on open communities such as Facebook, Twitter and other social media.

In two-way collaboration, consumers hence expect us to listen as well. Good research starts without asking questions. Open communities can be great places to find new consumer insights. Crowdsourcing initiatives deliver the seeds for a Consumer Consulting Board where ideas can be developed further in the community. Creating synergies between natural and research communities will be key. We applied this philosophy in our cooperation with 🗋 **Danone** R&D.[2] In order to further develop their formula milk offering, we first listened to what consumers were already saying about this topic on forums dedicated to infant feeding. This information was shared later on with the members of the Board. As a result, we could directly focus the discussion on closing the knowledge gaps.

Social media listening is not the only way in which we will recycle existing conversations. Consumers will come to the rescue here as well. The members of your Consumer Consulting Board will go searching for insights on open platforms for you. They can act as journalists reporting back on the bigger social media space. They are the most powerful algorithm there is that can easily deal

159

with big amounts of information. They can easily adapt to the visual revolution thanks to the popularity of platforms such as Instagram, Pinterest or Vine. But above all, they will select those stories from natural platforms that are relevant for your brand. They will become your eyes and ears in the online world.

There is
no way back

Consumers love to collaborate with brands. But they do not think in silos. They will not restrict their collaboration only to the areas we ask their cooperation for. A full engagement means that they will help out in areas where we do not involve consumers yet. Today they already help out in customer service by giving advice to peers or do pre-sales

by recommending products on social media. **Walmart** is even investigating whether they can outsource part of their distribution to consumers who are ordering online. We will increasingly outsource tasks to consumers that where never considered to be outsourced before.

Let's start with our own industry. Our community participants already help us with moderation, interpretation and contextualizing of the research results. But what about fully outsourcing the analysis of results to consumers or moving to real consumer consultancy where consumers will help to shape and adapt marketing models?

As Consumer Consulting Boards are relatively new, many of them have not reached full maturity yet. Engagement on the side of both the brand and the consumer will only grow. We can expect a whole new dynamic in the communities of the future. We predict that

160

consumers will increasingly take the lead within the Consumer Consulting Board. They will not wait to get activated by a newsletter or new challenge on the community. As a real member of the boardroom, they will put topics on the table and as such guide the community themselves. We will see the rise of the consumer employee, already coined today as the *Insumer*.[3] They will be involved in executing some of the decisions made in the community on the Board. Tasks will be outsourced to the community. The company network will be extended with the Consumer Consulting Board network. Agility will get a new meaning in rapid prototyping or crowdfunding.

Consumer Consulting Boards will become the central nervous system of the organization. '*Always-on, always right*', they will be involved in a wider range of decisions. Silos between the departments will vanish as the consumer employees will not only advise marketing departments but also give consulting on attracting new workforces (HR), boosting your sales, ... More direct interaction between brands and consumers can be expected. This interaction will take place through a variety of channels: on the community, marketers will directly address consumers. Through video conferencing consumers will be able to give input during certain meetings. Meet & greets in real life will become a natural extension of the online platform. As researchers, we will take up a role in facilitating and moderating this brand engagement.

We do not know if all of this will become reality, but one thing is for sure: the future of research communities looks bright! They will remain an exciting playground for researchers, consumers and clients. In this new ecosystem, triangulation will be key. The cosmopolitan consumer will be grasped by a combination of research techniques and devices which tackle the same issue from different angles. Only through a mix of implicit and explicit techniques we will be able to understand the rational, emotional and conative (behavioural) consumer. Consumers will play a role as journalists. They will become full members of the board of companies and report to us about their life and environment. This new ecosystem will allow marketers to have a continuous dialogue where the consumer is available 24/7 to help out. Isn't this exciting?

Staying **ahead**
of the curve

by Thomas Troch & Anouk Willems

With trends like *life caching*, *the employee consumer* and *fusion research* respectively coming from the world of consumers, business and marketing research, communities are in a continuous evolution to match the changing needs and expectations of all stakeholders. Although the goal of a Consumer Consulting Board is to engage in a structural collaboration with consumers, the approach is very adaptive and far from rigid. By working in different waves, a new wave can easily be customized to engage new stakeholders in the company (additional departments) or to change the focus; getting close to your consumer, uncovering new insights, developing new ideas and concepts or driving customer experience and action. These adaptations are not only steered top-down from the company's perspective; participants' spontaneous conversations can challenge the scope along the way. Empowered

....

'The encouraging words of the moderator are really great. By stimulating us to start our own discussions in the social corner and highlighting the most interesting ones, we really feel we have an impact on the community.'

Ljm_angel69 of Walk the Talk

....

consumers do not hesitate to share their feedback on the topics that are placed on the agenda.

Our job is never done

Although every Consumer Consulting Board is uniquely fitted to the organization, some changes and best practices are relevant to all Boards as they have an impact on the methodology of research communities. The ForwaR&D Lab at InSites Consulting is the driving force behind the development of fresh and powerful tools to connect consumers with the brands and categories they are involved with. To keep ahead of the curve, they are reaching out to all stakeholders to create, refine and rigorously test new research approaches that add value to clients and consumers as well as research consultants. Most of these R&D insights are the unique result of a co-created effort involving different stakeholders who share an interest in taking research forward:

- Our clients, ensuring that our innovations provide new and better answers to real problems and challenges they are faced with.
- Our research participants, helping us to align our methodology and software to their expectations in order to provide an engaging experience, resulting in richer data.

163

- Our team, sharing ideas and best practices as they come along on a daily basis and more structurally , in monthly co-creation sessions.
- Our *Global Community Moderator and Consumer Co-researcher Networks*, driving local relevance and ensuring a user-centric approach.
- Academic partners, enabling us to collaborate with the sharpest minds in marketing theory (e.g. IESEG School of Management, University of Maastricht, University of Wageningen, University of Nijmegen, Vlerick Business School). More in particular, the dynamics of online conversations and its implications for communities have been a key research area in the PhD dissertation of **Stephan Ludwig** at the **University of Maastricht**, financially supported by InSites Consulting.

By involving all of our stakeholders, we are walking our own talk in applying the same principles of being *open* and *agile* to the ongoing development of Consumer Consulting Boards. This holistic view allows improvements on three levels;[4] doing things more efficiently, going further and digging deeper and finally doing things that were not possible before.

Doing things more efficiently

Recession can prompt unusual levels of creativity; research faces constraints to deliver more impactful results within a shorter timeframe and lower budget. There is a need to tap into the opportunities provided by new technological tools and take maximum advantage of the researchers' skills by crossing the discipline's boundaries. The end of ad hoc research is near, making room for structural consumer collaboration and allowing companies to be agile whilst protecting cost efficiency. A research community will help employees to make decisions more rapidly; next to their gut feeling they can also consult non-stop feedback of consumers.

By using a logic similar to social platforms such as Facebook, the members of the Consumer Consulting Board can intuitively find their way around the portal and focus on what really matters; sharing their stories and joining the discussions. Integrated analysis tools allow the consultant to structure the information during the moderation and quickly share the highlights with clients. In addition to the original discussions and multimedia output, a customized communication approach helps the

The Moderator Square

brand team focus on the findings that can really make a difference. To further increase the efficiency and thus the time for value-adding activities such as moderation, interpretation and analysis, an intensive collaboration with community managers is set up.

- **The Moderator Square**

    As you could read in the third chapter, selecting, training and certifying our external community moderators is not the end… It is only the beginning of a relationship in which we can learn from each other and shape the future of online qualitative research together. Therefore, we have created a platform for connecting and collaborating with all the members of our *Global Community Moderator Network*: the *Moderator Square*.

- **Co-creating with our moderators**

    Next to some practical pages, a blog and a social corner, the most important part of the *Moderator Square* is the *co-create* corner. In this corner we are discussing topics such as the impact of cultural differences on running research communities. We are not limiting ourselves to moderation only, but also trigger a deep dive into recruitment, processes, timings and incentives. This co-creation community allows us to tap into the rich experience of moderators all over the world, making our research locally relevant. The learnings of these topics are being shared on the

Moderator Square and during our annual *Consumer Consulting Board Festival*: an online conference where the complete network is invited to submit abstracts for presentations. Key findings also serve as material for our papers, webinars and speeches at congresses.

- **Continuous learning**

    Via the *Moderator Square* we keep our moderators up-to-speed on all recent developments, studies and learnings, so we are able to plug them into our projects efficiently. However, the main thing is to learn from them and tap into their experience and local knowledge to make our research locally relevant. Via the *i-deate corner*, our external moderators can launch their ideas on how to improve efficiency and make our processes and practices better. But on a project basis as well, we involve our local moderators early in the process, so they can immediately integrate their local knowledge into our projects, for example by giving us input on locally relevant incentives, helping us with finding the right local recruitment partners for very specific profiles, or by making sure all communication has the right tone of voice and style that will encourage the members to participate.

- **Moderator Square, the inside story**

    The internal counter-part of the *Moderator Square* are the so-called *Take a coffee & learn* sessions. These monthly workshop sessions with the

165

InSites Consulting community managers team create a platform where they share experiences and come up with solutions to problem situations. The briefing of our software development, amongst others, is based on these sessions, and by bundling all experiences, the efficiency of our qualitative analysis can be optimized.

Going further and digging deeper

The asynchronous and longitudinal connection with consumers builds mutual trust and provides a true understanding of their habits, emotions and perceptions. The creation of an engaging participant experience benefits the gathered information; discussions excel in number of comments, length of stories and richness by multimedia integration.

Our Walk the Talk community

The participant experience is enforced by applying multiple methods - storytelling, projective techniques, short questionnaires, ethnography, ... - and integrating a Facebook and a mobile application to access the Consumer Consulting Board. But we can always do better! By structurally involving the most active community members in the development of the methodology, it can be adapted to changing expectations and new opportunities. Adoption of social tools such as Instagram and Pinterest, for example, also has an influence on how we can engage participants to share more pictures.

Taking the participant experience from good to great

- **The Participant Consulting Board**
  To start a dialogue with consumers participating in research we gather some of the most inspirational Consumer Consulting Board members in a community... about communities: the *Walk the Talk community*! By getting to know them better and gaining insight in the way they want to start up a dialogue with brands, we can increase their involvement. The participants' involvement and enthusiasm have a major impact on the quality and richness of the discussions. The objectives are very similar to the ones of a typical Consumer Consulting Board: from getting close to participants to developing solutions. This

Consumer Consulting Board is being reactivated at key moments throughout the year to continuously gain insight into their perception of changes, test software updates and improve overall communication.

- **Driving participant experience & co-creating solutions**
We apply a similar approach to the development of our software as we do to the pre-launch of digital services for our clients. Our ideation tool has been developed to anticipate the need of consumers to share their ideas with us. Through several iterations, the *Walk the Talk* community was sharing ideas on how to approach co-creation and they have tested several versions of the tool before it was rolled out on all platforms. One of the key insights was that participants perceive the practice of developing ideas as a collaborative effort. To intrinsically stimulate co-creation, the tool is not granting a gamification status to individual participants, but to ideas. As participants comment on each others' ideas, they get better and level up from mining to rough diamond, polished diamond and eventually a diamond ring. Another example is the idea of integrating Facebook-like notifications on the community, a feature which will be included in a future version of the platform.

'I'd rather not receive numerous e-mails containing the odd update, but instead receive 1 clear and structured mail. But when you see what a community entails for a brand, it gives satisfaction and simply makes you want to participate even more! :-)'

Leuven21 of Walk the Talk

Ideation badges: from 'mining' ideas to finished 'jewels'

Doing things that were just not possible before

By connecting for a longer time span with consumers through a Consumer Consulting Board, the knowledge which is gained in a first stage can be applied immediately, which automatically gives the discussions more depth. As not only the consumers but the client's team also has access to the community during this longer time span, the boundaries of the departments in the organization will fade away, an interdisciplinary collaboration will emerge and teams will be able to make decisions faster and with more confidence. This co-creation approach stimulates the development of new concepts and reinforces the activities between the brand and its consumers.

Collaboration with clients

To truly create an impact through such a consumer connection, the approach needs to be integrated seamlessly in a company's processes. And although there is room for ongoing improvements, making a head start is crucial to make this a success. Therefore innovation projects in the *ForwaR&D Lab* are always set up based on a need that is relevant to our clients. By organizing regular co-creation workshops with clients we are actually

defining the topics for the research innovation funnel, comparing their needs and ideas with evolutions we spot in the world of consumers and marketing.

Research-on-research projects are often joined innovation efforts, where clients are taking a crucial role in challenging the status quo. Naturally the communication of results is one of the challenges where the research industry as a whole can still make a big leap forward. From engaging the **Unilever** [5] R&D workforce with games to providing inspiration to the **Heineken** design team [6] with an interactive infographic, the quest to inspire and engage different departments within the company with insightful content will never end. But we go beyond communication in this co-creation approach by challenging all boundaries of research.

A nice example is the paper we wrote together with **Air France and KLM** [7] on our quest to cross the boundaries of research. We moved beyond the boundaries of time by digging into the past at the start of the research project. By taking advantage of the longitudinal nature of communities we were not only able to create an impact faster but also in a better way. We went beyond the boundaries of methods by analyzing our data with a quantitative mind-set and taking advantage of (new) ways of measuring emotions implicitly. We left the boundaries of our profession behind by using best practices of related disciplines like advertising or journalism in the presentation of our results.

The Consumer Consulting Board does not only provide a structural connection to consumers, but also to the research team. Investing in this relationship is extremely beneficial for the impact of the research as consecutive learning effects - in terms of relevant analysis models and reporting formats - can customize the approach. We learn from each other in both ways, by immersing at the client side to understand the processes and by giving training to the client team so they can have a direct connection with the consumers on the community. When **Joëlla Marsman** changed focus within **H.J. Heinz**, she even started an internship at InSites Consulting to immerse in the world of consumer collaboration before taking on the role of dedicated community manager at H.J. Heinz.

Co-creating the future of Consumer Consulting Boards with clients

Adaptive
co-creation setting

To involve the different stakeholders in the best possible way, this is the adaptive co-creation setting the *ForwaR&D Lab* has developed. From these collaboration efforts we learn that co-creation with moderators, participants and clients can be translated into doing things more efficiently, going further and digging deeper and doing things that were not possible before. Of course their contributions are not limited to one of these objectives and the power of this co-creation setting lies in the cross-fertilization of ideas by the different stakeholders. New topics on our innovation agenda include advanced measurement of the impact of structural collaboration with consumers on organizations, demystifying sources and formats that trigger inspiration for creative minds and marketers and measuring the power of interaction in consumer discussions.

In addition to guiding the development of the communities as a methodology, we share these findings in the articles and presentations we submit to world-leading conferences. Over the past years, this has already resulted in more than 25 national and international awards. We're proud to showcase the awards we received on page 80.

169

TWEETAWAYS

The researcher of the future will need to be an expert in creative cutting, detecting patterns in the river of big data.
@annaliezze

Consumer Consulting Boards will become the central nerve system of an organization: always on, always right.
@anneliezze

The end of ad hoc research is near, making room for structural consumer collaboration.
@AnoukW1

Consumer Consulting Boards are an integral part of a brand's eco-system, creating synergies with internal and external branding.
@tomderuyck

Communities are no longer about technology. The future is to the ones who understand how to inspire business decisions and cultures.
@tomderuyck

THE BASICS OF CONSUMER CONSULTING BOARDS

A Consumer Consulting Board brings your consumers together on an online closed community to help shape your business. The end goal is structural collaboration, having a continuous dialogue with consumers that is 24/7, across departments and objectives.

Structural collaboration with customers is HOT!

83% of decision makers have one or want to build an research community this year [1]

8 out of 10 consumers want to collaborate with brands [2]

36% prefer this collaboration to take place in a branded research community [3]

The 4 pillars that underpin a Consumer Consulting Board

WHO?

People that are **interesting & interested!** Collaborate with people that have a specific profile. Fans of a specific brand or topic, revealing a high brand and/or topic identification.

HOW MANY?

To reach the saturation level of on-topic arguments at 30 posts per thread, we need between 50 and 150 participants. Depending on the objectives & duration, we can invite more members in different subgroups.

HOW LONG?

The community is set up for a long-term collaboration. The exact duration of the community depends on the objectives: ranging from 3 weeks to months, or even ongoing **24/7**.

WHY?

The community serves multiple objectives. We identify 4 types of objectives:
1/ Getting close to the consumer
2/ Uncover new insights
3/ Generate & craft ideas and concept
4/ Activating consumers

5 tips for going global:
cross the boundaries of space

1. Work with **native moderators** who speak the language and know the local cultures & market situation.

2. **Adapt the conversation guide.** Customize your questions and tasks to local cultures to get the most out of your members.

3. Play upon different **motivations and offer custom incentives** to adapt the community to local cultures.

5. **Play for attention.** Adjust your game thinking across countries.

4. **Go mobile,** as in most new markets it is the default screen/device to access the web.

5 TIPS FOR GOING GLOBAL CONSUMER CONSULTING BOARD CAN CROSS THE BOUNDARIES OF SPACE

How to leverage your Consumer Consulting Board?

Knowledge leverage

The Consumer Consulting Board needs to be an engaging experience to get the richest inspiration

MIX THE STORYLINE & TOOLS

Become a DJ and create the right **mix of different tasks, discussions and tools** (diary tasks, photo tasks, polls). Make your conversation guide a true story being told to the participants.

USE GAMIFICATION & FUN ELEMENTS

By integrating play mechanisms, participants **think harder** which leads up to **7x richer data**, but also **think differently** through emotional, contextual and creative techniques.

4 ways to create an engaging experience

MAKE IT MOBILE

Give members 24/7 access, through mobile applications to get **more contextual and personal data**.

COLLABORATE WITH CO-RESEARCHERS

Empower members to become co-researchers in moderation, interpretation and analyses which delivers up to **2x more interactive discussions, and up to 40% additional insights** and more to the point conclusions.

3 essential steps of change management for making
the Consumer Consulting Board impactful within the organization

Engage the internal
stakeholders with the
consumers by **immersing**
them in the consumer world.
Invite them to play consumer
games amongst others and
confront them with their current
knowledge gaps to create
positive disruption.

Inspire the internal
stakeholders with new
eye-openers and daily
sparks of inspiration from
the community. Support
interactive reporting through
the consumer platform and
collect questions to **close
knowledge gaps**.

Activate the internal
stakeholders by
translating results into
actions in workshops,
to enable agile **decision
making**. Create
materials that ensure
that the research is used
afterwards as well.

177

External leverage

Create impact outside the organization! 3 tips on how to communicate
about your Consumer Consulting Board

Communicate about the
process. Talk about the fact
that you have a Consumer
Consulting Board.

Communicate the outcome.
Show the (end) result(s) of the
collaboration: new products
or services co-created with
consumers.

Communicate about the
insights. Share the learnings
of the project.

The power of letting go: turning consumers into heroes

Throughout this book, we have stressed the need to empower your consumers to start collaborating with your teams, turning them into the real heroes as opposed to your brand. This concluding article acts as a short wrap-up of the book, highlighting why consumers are the best consultants any company can hire, what makes the Consumer Consulting Board so powerful, and how the future might look like.

There is a major change happening in marketing today, with the devastating force of a tsunami. The scary thing about a tsunami is that you do not see it coming until it is too late. Three underlying forces of change are at play. A first one is technological disruption. The digital revolution has dramatically changed the business context we are all operating in, making the world increasingly *open* and *transparent* and shifting power from organizations and brands to individuals and consumers. Existing business models become obsolete in a split second and the way we build businesses will never be the same again. Nothing, neither money nor power, really stands in the way of people to create their own reality from the environmental change around us. If you are talented and creative, you can make it happen. More than ever, brands need to be agile, adjusting to new realities much faster than they ever were able to.

'The big old institutions fought the Internet and the Internet won.'
Don Tapscott, CEO, The Tapscott Group
Author, Speaker and Consultant

Secondly, with one out of three global citizens being part of Generation Y, the *Millennials* are having a deep and profound impact on society at large. They expect brands to be truthful, transparent and open. They expect brands to involve them in the co-creation of their future. They are marketing-savvy, taking a critical look at how brands behave. They want to collaborate and associate with like-minded people to build their own unique brands out of the components that companies provide them with. Finally, we witness a gravitational shift in how society is further globalizing, with companies such as P&G and Unilever generating more than half of their revenues from the 'new' economies, that are catching up fast or even outpacing more mature and established markets. Brands need to become *universal*: adapting to different new cultures, but staying true to what they stand for.

The amplifying effect of all three forces of change combined really turns it into a tsunami: Millennials are the most mature generation when it comes to having access to and using the latest digital and mobile platforms and applications; in several emerging markets more than half of the population is aged under 30; digital technology is connecting people from anywhere across the globe, acting as a very convenient transmitter from mature markets to emerging ones and the other way round.

Consumer collaboration is moving into mainstream

We are all well aware of the quote: *'It is not the strongest of the species who survives nor the most intelligent one. It is the one who is the most adaptable to change.'* But how can or should organizations adapt to the current and ever accelerating change we see? Experts, futurists and trend watchers are teaming up to deep dive into what society will look like in 2020, how marketing should reinvent itself and what the impact is on organizational capabilities, structures and leadership. Looking at the forces of change mentioned above, extreme customer centricity will be an essential component of future success. More than ever, creating relevance for and through consumers is the key to unlocking and earning reach.

'Many old-school CEOs are stuck in their ways; we need more collaboration and openness.'
Paul Polman, CEO, Unilever

Organizations of the future will have learned to let go, tapping into the power and wisdom of people who are not on their payroll. Scanning through scientific articles, conference presentations and blog posts, we cannot escape the vast amount of terms such as *collaboration*,

openness, *empowerment* and *'transparency*' showing up. And this is not surprising at all. Embracing an outside-in perspective, and more specifically a consumer perspective, delivers the best chances to create relevance for those consumers. By listening to and involving a hybrid group of interested and interesting consumers, we get to novel and rich ideas for the future. Compared to other groups, consumer crowds are the most intrinsically motivated, making it also a very efficient process of creating new value. Can you imagine any company paying a salary to an employee who is just hanging around, waiting for a problem that will need solving? In short: collaboration with consumers is moving into mainstream, and even if you do not take advantage of it, your competitors will surely will.

'Crowdsourcing is the only way you can be successful. Everyone in the company benefits from decentralizing the decision-making process.'
Tony Hsieh, CEO, Zappos

Some battles have been won, but the war is far from over

That being said, several experts still consider the current situation comparable to *teenage sex*: *'Everybody is talking about it, few are doing it and only a couple are good at it!'* There seems to be a clear paradox here: while there is ample evidence we are in the midst of a perfect storm to lift on the benefits of collaborating with consumers, organizations are relatively slow in adopting collaborative methods.

Editorial team: Kristof De Wulf & Tom De Ruyck

Despite a growing list of successful cases (for a great overview, check out the timeline of crowdsourcing by the world's best brands), only a minority of companies have structurally embedded consumers into their value creation process.

'Above all else, align with customers. Win when they win. Win only when they win.'

Jeff Bezos, CEO, Amazon

Today's consumers have unlimited opportunities to shout out to brands what they think, but only a minority of brands are actually *hard listening* to them, translating listening into actual hearing and acting. Managers remain understandably cautious and relatively little evidence is available that takes away doubts about the potential business impact. Several questions pop up when considering involving *strangers* or everyday people in

helping your brand succeed in an ever complex world: what about intellectual property, the question how to involve the right kind of collaborators, what about the costs, how can idea leaks be prevented, when do crowds outperform the internal organization and when not, what kind of problems or tasks can be handled effectively and efficiently by consumer crowds? While this book touches on quite some evidence already, there is still a long road ahead of us.

The Consumer Consulting Board

The questions above typically emerge in open collaboration and co-creation settings. Openness typically implies a lack of *cohesiveness*, *coordination* and *control*. The Consumer Consulting Board is different given its closed nature. It is customized towards the culture and structure of an organization, it is actively moderated and managed, the participating board members are deliberately selected and refreshed, and dissemination of consumer input is optimally facilitated throughout the organization in a structured way. It offers an environment that blends the loose, open and decentralized character of open collaboration initiatives with the necessary coordination, focus and expert knowledge to make it truly relevant and powerful for your organization.

'Put customers in the driver's seat, or be dead by 2020.'
Jamie Nordstrom, EVP, Nordstrom

Nevertheless, before getting involved in a structural collaboration with consumers, it is a good idea for organizations to take a close look in the mirror. How open is your company culture today and are you ready to take it to the next level? Ultimately, the Consumer Consulting Board is there to make your consumers feel like insiders and your insiders like consumers. It takes guts to get there.

Towards a collaborative business eco-system

Ultimately, organizations will need to learn how different stakeholders can naturally interact with each other and create corporate value, with various crowds of people becoming fixed institutions that are available on demand or provide support without even being asked for it. In other words, they will need to think of building a collabora-

tive eco-system that is balanced, that limits waste to a minimum and that uses output from one collaboration source as input for another. In order to make this happen, a strong corporate vision is essential, offering a clear framework and focus for collaboration through a set of shared values and objectives. Ultimately, the collaborative eco-system means a radical transformation of the way organizations function, bridging internal silos and inviting a more diverse set of actors in creating and delivering value.

'The power of everyday people is driving monumental change'
Marc Pritchard, CMO, P&G

The future is bright and exciting. The era of consumer hierarchy is upon us and we will see more and more brands *for the people, by the people*. We hope you enjoyed reading this book and were able to derive new inspiration for your own organization and brand. We only just started this fascinating journey and, as you know, we never consider our job to be done. Thanks to our ForwaR&D Lab, we will continue to go beyond the boundaries and add to the existing body of evidence. We want to express a big thank you to everyone who has walked together with us so far, with a special thanks to our clients who were so bold as to take the first steps into this new territory.

Kristof De Wulf
Tom De Ruyck

181

About
InSites Consulting

InSites Consulting is a new-generation agency stretching the boundaries of marketing research. Being recognized as one of the most innovative companies in market research (GRIT report 2012), we love taking things forward and have been doing so for the last 15 years.

Taking research forward

Marketing research is still at the very core of what we do. That being said, we stretch the boundaries of research, exploring new territories to drive value for our clients. We believe that consumers are the most effective consultants for any company. By empowering them, we unlock their consulting potential and make brands future-proof. On our journey to take research forward, we have been cheered by the industry with more than 25 international awards so far.

Taking marketing forward

Research is a means to an end. Ultimately, it is about making a meaningful difference in your market, driving relevance for consumers and helping brands grow. In everything we do, we take a consultative approach. That is why we write books about what it means to be successful as a brand in today's marketing era. That is why

we inspire our clients to engage and collaborate creatively with customers in order to shape the future of their brands. That is why we start projects from a deep understanding of our clients' challenges via our dedicated sector teams.

Taking clients forward

We are blessed to have the chance to work with more than 35% of the best global brands out there (Interbrand, 2012). Brands that understand that new approaches are needed to remain successful. Brands that seek new growth opportunities outside of their core home markets. Brands that embrace the idea that consumers need to be involved in defining and crafting their future.

Taking ourselves forward

We are a crazy blend of academic visionaries, passionate marketers and research innovators who are determined to challenge the status quo. Over the last 10 years, we have grown at an amazing 25% a year. Today, more than 125 enthusiasts working in five offices (New York, Timisoara, London, Rotterdam and Ghent) get their energy from helping world-leading brands to develop deeper connections with consumers on a global scale. We live by our forward values every single day: Forward, Open, Result-driven, We-oriented, Adaptive, Respectful and Daring.

Some of our pioneering clients

Anke Moerdyck

Marketing Manager

Project manager

🐦 @Anke_InSites

in be.linkedin.com/in/ankemoerdyck/

✉ anke.moerdyck@insites-consulting.com

Anke joined InSites Consulting in 2006 after studying Communication Management in Ghent. In her current role as Marketing Manager, she's mainly responsible for the corporate brand & communication, press relations and marketing strategy. Over the years, Anke has contributed to numerous successful marketing initiatives at InSites Consulting: the (re)branding of the InSites Consulting Smartees events, the communication and branding of publications such as The Conversation Company, the Social Media around the World study, How Cool Brands Stay Hot and many more.

Anne-Laure Simoens

Senior Client Operations Executive

Copy editor

✉ anne-laure.simoens@insites-consulting.com

Anne-Laure is Senior Client Operations Executive. She is responsible for the coordination of various internal and external services: translations and proofreading, quality checks of online and offline documents and surveys, preparation of questionnaires for IT implementation and coding of open-ended answers. She has a master's degree in translations and has been working in the world of market research since 1996. She joined InSites Consulting early 2009 and is actively involved in the expansion of the quality department.

Anneleen Boullart

Research Consultant

Co-author

🐦 @AnneleenBoullar
💼 be.linkedin.com/in/anneleenboullart
✉ anneleen.boullart@insites-consulting.com

Annelies Verhaeghe

Head of Research Innovation

Co-author

🐦 @annaliezze
💼 be.linkedin.com/in/anneliesverhaeghe
✉ annelies.verhaeghe@insites-consulting.com

185

Freshly graduated as a Master in Marketing Management, Anneleen joined InSites Consulting in 2011 as a Qualitative Research Consultant, focusing on research communities. She is a dedicated member of the media & entertainment team and she managed numerous communities, both short-term (AT&T, Dorel) and continuous (Famous, H.J. Heinz). Anneleen is focusing on both local and global projects and she's also engaged in R&D-related projects (e.g. she conducted an in-depth qualitative research about online research communities in the BRIC countries). Furthermore she's co-author of the 'No guts, no glory' publication, together with Joeri Van den Bergh. She interviewed close to 20 international marketers about Generation Y in order to define the dos and don'ts when communicating with or doing marketing towards this generation. Next to that, Anneleen shares her knowledge with a broader audience through presentations about mobile marketing and gamification at HoGent.

Annelies is Head of Research Innovation. She is passionate about consumer insights and neo-observational research techniques such as multimedia ethnography and social media netnography. In 2009, Annelies won the ESOMAR Young Researcher of the Year award with her paper on aging 'And they lived happily ever after', using social media netnography and co-creation to better understand how health conditions can affect the elderly and their care givers. Besides that, Annelies has been a regular speaker at international marketing research and technology events. And as an influential blogger, she has contributed to several publications in academic and trade journals. Next to her role as research innovator, Annelies is also in charge of the InSites Consulting office in Timisoara, Romania.

Anouk Willems

Research Innovation Manager

Co-author

🐦 @AnoukW1

in nl.linkedin.com/in/anoukwillems

✉ anouk.willems@insites-consulting.com

Els Cocquyt

Community Moderator Network Manager

Co-author

🐦 @redalert888

in be.linkedin.com/in/elscocquyt

✉ els.cocquyt@insites-consulting.com

With an education in marketing and a passion for co-creation, Anouk connects brands with consumers through research communities. After having managed communities for global clients like Unilever, H.J. Heinz and eBay, she is now part of the InSites Consulting ForwaR&D lab. In her current role, Anouk focuses on innovating the community solutions and exploring new opportunities in the mobile domain and using co-researcher techniques. She specializes in consumer immersion solutions and branding & activation projects. She founded an online platform on DIY, called 'Klusopedia' (Dutch) about 4 years ago and she has great affinity with online marketing and social media. Anouk is a frequent speaker at marketing research conferences and has been awarded for her work by ESOMAR with the Best Presentation Award at the ESOMAR 3D Digital Dimensions 2012.

Els started her career about 10 years ago in a recruitment agency specialized in qualitative research. In 2008 she joined InSites Consulting where she is managing and experiencing the growth of online qualitative research in all its forms: online discussion groups, ethnography, web-facilitated interviews and of course research communities. With InSites Consulting expanding its horizon and conducting qualitative research on a global scale, she became an expert in the recruitment of qualitative freelance consultants. She is focusing on the ongoing recruitment and management of the InSites Consulting Global Community Moderator Network, making sure all our moderators stay up-to-date on new projects, technologies, specific trainings, etc.

Hakim Zemni

Managing Director Belgium

Co-author

🐦 @HakimZemni

in be.linkedin.com/in/hakimzemni

✉ hakim.zemni@insites-consulting.com

Hakim is Managing Director and Corporate Business Director of Media & Entertainment. He has been active in market research and marketing since 1998 and is a specialist in content management of integrated qualitative and quantitative online market research. Hakim's expertise areas today are media, popular culture, qualitative analysis and moderation, consumer understanding and brand positioning. He has been a guest speaker at numerous international seminars, workshops, events and congresses throughout his 15 years of marketing and research expertise. He has a master's degree in Communication Sciences.

Hannes Willaert

Head of Design

Design

in be.linkedin.com/in/hanneswillaert

✉ hannes.willaert@insites-consulting.com 187

As Head of Design, Hannes is in charge of all internal and external design processes such as branding material, presentations, corporate identity and much more. Having a broad interest in aesthetics in terms of graphic design, architecture and interior design, Hannes co-founded Cookie Collective a few years ago, a small graphic design company that has already been working with InSites Consulting since a number of years. Later on, Hannes joined InSites Consulting as a full-time designer. In the meantime, he keeps on running Cookie Collective as a secondary profession. Next to that, Hannes is also on the jury of the final projects of VISO students (a graphic design school located in Ghent).

Joeri Van den Bergh

Co-founder & Gen Y expert

Co-author

🐦 @Joeri_InSites

in be.linkedin.com/in/joerivandenbergh

✉ joeri.vandenbergh@insites-consulting.com

Joeri is co-founder of and managing partner. In his main domains - marketing communications, branding and consumer behavior - he has published several marketing books, such as the AMA Marketing Book of The Year 2012 'How Cool Brands Stay Hot, Branding to Generation Y'. This bestselling key title of Kogan Page has been translated into 7 languages and is globally recognized by both marketing executives and academic experts. Joeri's research papers have been published in academic media such as Journal of Advertising and International Journal of Consumer Marketing and got featured in business media such as Forbes, USA Today and Chicago Tribune. His keynote speeches on Gen Y marketing and branding were applauded around the world, from Las Vegas over Toronto to Manila. With his consumer insights he has inspired global brands in various industries, such as PepsiCo, DIESEL, MasterCard, Yamaha and Absolut. More info on Joeri, his books and Generation Y on: www.howcoolbrandsstayhot.com

Kristof De Wulf, PhD

CEO & Co-founder

Co-author and final editor

🐦 @kristofdewulf

in be.linkedin.com/in/dewulfkristof

✉ kristof.dewulf@insites-consulting.com

Kristof started at the Vlerick Business School, obtaining a PhD in Applied Economic Sciences and later becoming Associate Marketing Professor and Partner at the same business school. Together with 3 Vlerick colleagues, Kristof co-founded InSites Consulting in 1997, acting as CEO of the company since 2012, providing strategic direction and energy to the 5 teams and more than 125 employees. With over 20 years of relevant experience with world-leading FMCG brands, Kristof is still very much involved in supporting clients. He is account director for PepsiCo, Mars, Danone and Unilever, helping them unlock the consulting potential that resides in 'ordinary' consumers. Kristof has published numerous articles in academic journals, business books and trade magazines. In 2010, he has been awarded with the MOA Agency Researcher of the year award. He is a regular speaker at various marketing research events worldwide. He is included in 'The Ultimate List of Social CEOs on Twitter', just a few places behind Oprah Winfrey, Richard Branson and Rupert Murdoch :-).

Liesbeth Dambre

Project Resource Manager

Co-author

@LiesbethDambre

be.linkedin.com/in/liesbethdambre/

liesbeth.dambre@insites-consulting.com

Liesbeth is in charge of all external resources used for InSites Consulting projects. Liesbeth started her career as a quantitative research consultant and has supported the InSites Consulting growth by streamlining processes & leading numerous quality projects in the function of Quality Manager. In the past year, in her new role of Project Resource Manager, she has been in charge of building and managing the Global Community Moderator Network, managing our own TalkToChange research panel and all other project supplier relationships.

Natalie Mas

Marketing Operations Executive

Co-author

@MasNatalie

be.linkedin.com/in/nataliemas

natalie.mas@insites-consulting.com

Graduated as a Master after Master in Multilingual Business Communication, Natalie joined the InSites Consulting Marketing team in 2012. Having a broad interest in market research and marketing, Natalie already spent some time at InSites Consulting in 2012 during a 4 month internship, contributing to a lot of R&D and marketing projects. Her interests in the field of qualitative market research in general and research communities in particular have led to this being the main theme of her master dissertation about structural collaboration and the shift from collaboration to communication within a company, based on in-depth interviews with marketers from Heineken, H.J. Heinz, Vodafone and many more. In her current role as Marketing Operations Executive, she is mainly responsible for the company's conversation management, the organization of InSites Consulting Smartees events and the support of all internal and external communication flows.

Niels Schillewaert, PhD

Managing Partner and Co-founder

Co-author

🐦 @niels_insites

in linkedin.com/in/nielsschillewaert

✉ niels.schillewaert@insites-consulting.com

Thomas Troch

Research Innovation Manager

Co-author

🐦 @thomastroch

in be.linkedin.com/in/thomastroch

✉ thomas.troch@insites-consulting.com

Niels is co-founder of and Managing Partner. Niels is based in the US office where he manages client projects for e.g. MasterCard, Coca-Cola, AB InBev, AT&T and Pernod Ricard. He was a Professor of Marketing at the Vlerick Business School and is an ISBM Research Fellow at PennState University (US). Niels was awarded several times for his research, is a frequent speaker at international conferences and a Council member of ESOMAR. His work was published in leading scientific journals such as Journal of Marketing, The International Journal of Research in Marketing, Journal of Services Research, Journal of the Academy of Marketing Science, Industrial Marketing Management, The Journal of Business Research, Survey Research Methods and Information & Management.

With a background in industrial design and a passion to understand people, Thomas connects brands with their consumers through new techniques like research communities. After managing research projects for global clients such as Unilever, Philips, Heineken and Vodafone, he is now focusing on the role of lead users in the innovation funnel. Thomas develops solutions to shape consumer insights and translate them into relevant ideas and concepts. He specializes in co-creation and service design projects. Thomas is a regular contributor to the research and design community by speaking at a variety of conferences, contributing to numerous journals and by lecturing on consumer-centric innovation at universities. He was recently awarded with the Best Presentation award at the 8th International Conference on Design and Emotion. Next to that, as a board member of The Fringe Factory, Thomas is also aiming to attract talented graduates into the research industry.

Tom De Ruyck

Head of Consumer Consulting Boards

Co-author and final editor

🐦 @tomderuyck

in be.linkedin.com/in/tomderuyck

✉ tom.deruyck@insites-consulting.com

Tom is in charge of InSites Consulting's global activities in terms of community research: thought leadership, steering innovation and business development. He has given more than 200 speeches around the world at major international marketing, research and technology conferences. Tom published several white papers as well as articles in academic journals, business books and trade magazines. Besides that, he is an influential blogger/tweeter on social media, industry trends and research communities. He was awarded for his work by the American Marketing Association (4 under 40: Emerging Leader of the Industry Award 2010), the MRS (ResearchLive Tweeter of the Year 2011) and the CMO Council USA & Asia (Leadership Award for Contribution to Market Research 2012). Next to his work at InSites Consulting, Tom is Adjunct Professor at IESEG School of Management (Lille, France) & EHSAL Management School (Brussels, Belgium). He is also co-founder & President of the Belgian research association BAQMaR.

Wim De Wever

Project & Method Manager

Co-author

🐦 @wimdewever

in be.linkedin.com/in/wimdewever

✉ wim.dewever@insites-consulting.com

Wim is Project & Method Manager in the domain of research communities and other qualitative research solutions (such as ethno research, online discussion groups and web facilitated interviews). He joined InSites Consulting in 2007 and has a wide variety of experience across all practical aspects of both quantitative and qualitative online research, mainly in close collaboration with the R&D department. In 2011, he co-established the formal position of the 'Project & Method Manager' function, a central function in the organization. In his role, Wim focuses on method & operational quality management. Firstly, he's being responsible for the continuous process and quality maintenance & innovation. Secondly, he acts as a change agent within the organization, bringing all internal stakeholders up to speed of changes efficiently and effectively. And thirdly, he serves as an internal account manager, taking full project management accountability for all implementation phases within the scope of the most complex projects.

References

Introduction

1   Greenbook Research Industry Trends Report. (2013). Retrieved from http://www.greenbookblog.org/grit

Chapter 1: What people expect from brands today

1   Trendwatching. (2013). Retrieved from http://trendwatching.com

2   eMarketer (2013). Brand Social Outreach Must Walk a Fine Line. Retrieved from http://www.emarketer.com/Article/Brand-Social-Outreach-Must-Walk-Fine-Line/1009712

3   Neff, J. (2013). Buzzkill: Coca-Cola Finds No Sales Lift from Online Chatter. AdAge Global. Retrieved from http://adage.com/article/cmo-strategy/coca-cola-sees-sales-impact-online-buzz-digital-display-effective-tv/240409

4   Nambisan, S. & Baron, R. (2009). Virtual Customer Environments: Testing a Model on Voluntary Participation in Value Creation Activities. Journal of Product Innovation Management, 26, 388-406.

5   Howe, J. (2008). Why the power of the crowd is driving the future of business. New York: Crown Publishing Group.

6   Howe, J. (2008). Why the power of the crowd is driving the future of business. New York: Crown Publishing Group.

7   Leadbeater, C. (2009). We think: mass innovation, not mass production. London: Profile Books Ltd.

8   My Starbucks Idea. (2013). Retrieved from http://www.mystarbucksidea.com

9   Van Belleghem, S. & De Ruyck, T. (2012). From Co-creation to Structural Collaboration: 5 pillars for structural collaboration with your customers. InSites Consulting Publication.

10   Van Belleghem, S., De Ruyck, T. & Thijs, D. (2012). Social Media around the World. InSites Consulting Publication.

Chapter 2: From co-creation to structural collaboration

1   Van Belleghem, S., De Ruyck, T. & Thijs, D. (2012). Social Media around the World. InSites Consulting Publication.

2   Van den Bergh, J. & Behrer, M. (2011). How Cool Brands Stay Hot: Branding to Generation Y. London: Kogan Page.

3   Schillewaert, N., De Ruyck, T., Van Kesteren, M. & Ludwig, S. (2010). How Fans became Future Shapers of an Ice-cream Brand: towards the next frontier in conducting insight communities. ESOMAR Qualitative Congress.

4   Willems, A., Schillewaert, N. & De Ruyck, T. (2013). Always-on Research. InSites Consulting Publication.

5   De Ruyck, T. et al. (2012). Designing the Club of Tomorrow: Consumer Understanding Guiding Creativity towards Success. ESOMAR General Congress.

6   Van Belleghem, S. & De Ruyck, T. (2012). From Co-creation to Structural Collaboration: 5 pillars for structural collaboration with your customers. InSites Consulting Publication.

7   Schillewaert, N. et al. (2011). The Dark Side of Crowdsourcing in Online Research Communities. CASRO Journal, 5-10.

8   De Ruyck, T. et al. (2011). Engage, Inspire, Act: 3 Step Stones towards Developing more Impactful Products. ESOMAR General Congress.

9   De Ruyck, T. & Veris E. (2011). Play, Interpret Together, Play again and Create a Win-win-win. ESOMAR 3D Congress.

10 De Ruyck, T. et al. (2011). Engage, Inspire, Act: 3 Step Stones towards Developing more Impactful Products. ESOMAR General Congress.

11 De Ruyck, T. et al. (2012). Designing the Club of Tomorrow: Consumer Understanding Guiding Creativity towards Success. ESOMAR General Congress.

12 De Ruyck, T. et al. (2011). Engage, Inspire, Act: 3 Step Stones towards Developing more Impactful Products. ESOMAR General Congress.

13 Luke, M. et al. (2012). Come Dine with Me, Australia. AMSRS National Conference.

14 Willems, A., De Ruyck, T. & Schillewaert, N. (2013). What Happens if Community Members Start Acting as Researchers. Quirk's Magazine.

15 Van Belleghem, S. & De Ruyck, T. (2012). From Co-creation to Structural Collaboration: 5 pillars for structural collaboration with your customers. InSites Consulting Publication.

16 Troch, T. et al. (2012). Doing More with Less: Crossing the Boundaries of Qualitative to Increase Business Impact. ESOMAR Qualitative Congress.

17 De Ruyck, T. et al. (2011). Engage, Inspire, Act: 3 Step Stones towards Developing more Impactful Products. ESOMAR General Congress.

18 De Ruyck, T. et al. (2011). Engage, Inspire, Act: 3 Step Stones towards Developing more Impactful Products. ESOMAR General Congress.

19 De Ruyck, T. et al. (2012). Designing the Club of Tomorrow: Consumer Understanding Guiding Creativity towards Success. ESOMAR General Congress.

20 De Ruyck, T. & Veris E. (2011). Play, Interpret Together, Play again and Create a Win-win-win. ESOMAR 3D Congress.

21 Van Belleghem, S., De Ruyck, T. & Thijs, D. (2012). Social Media Around the World. InSites Consulting Publication.

22 Deci, E. & Ryan, R. (1985). Intrinsic motivation and self-determination in human behavior. New York: Plenum Press.

23 Deutskens, E. (2006). From paper-and-pencil to screen-and-keyboard: studies on the Effectiveness of Internet-Based Marketing Research, 77-118.

24 Greenbook Research Industry Trends Report (2013). Retrieved from http://www.greenbookblog.org/grit

1   Cook, S. (2008). The Contribution Revolution: Letting Volunteers Build Your Business. Harvard Business Review, 86(10), 60-69.

2   Von Hippel, E. (1986). Lead Users: A Source of Novel Product Concepts. Management Science, 32(7), 791-806.

3   Peters, A. (2012). From Insight to Foresight. RW Connect.

4   Verhaeghe, A. et al. (2011). Crowd Interpretation: are participants the researchers of the future? ESOMAR General Congress.

5   Von Hippel, E. (1986). Lead Users: A Source of Novel Product Concepts. Management Science, 32(7), 791-806.

6   Rogers, E. (2003). Diffusion of innovations. New York: Free Press.

7   Andersson, J. (Interview). Esprit. 19 March 2012.

Chapter 4: Making global brands locally relevant

1   Severin, C. et al. (2011). Finding profits and growth in emerging markets. Retrieved from http://csi.mckinsey.com/Home/Knowledge_by_region/Global/Finging_profits_and_growth_in_emerging_markets.aspx

2   Linking population, poverty and development. (2007). Retrieved from http://www.unfpa.org/pds/urbanization.htm

3   United Nations, Department of Economic and Social Affairs, Population Division (2011). Retrieved from http://esa.un.org/wpp/population-pyramids/population-pyramids.htm

4   Bloomberg Markets (2013). The Top 20 Emerging Markets. Retrieved from http://www.bloomberg.com/slideshow/2013-01-30/the-top-20-emerging-markets.html

5   Kharas, H. (2010). The Emerging Middle Class in Developing Countries. Oecd development Centre Working Paper No. 285. Retrieved from http://www.oecd.org/dev/44457738.pdf

6   Van Belleghem, S., De Ruyck, T. & Thijs, D. (2012). Social Media around the World. InSites Consulting Publication.

7   Kaur, S. (2012). Strategy and Repositioning the Brand McDonald's in India. International Journal of Scientific and Research Publications, 2(9), 1-5.

8   Wentz, L. (2011). Johnnie Walker 'Rock Giant' Awakens Sleeping Colossus Brazil. AdAge Global. Retrieved from http://adage.com/article/global-news/johnnie-walker-awakens-sleeping-colossus-brazil-spot/230319/

9   Dupuis, C. (2007). The Iceberg Model of Culture. Retrieved from http://ebookbrowse.com/the-iceberg-model-of-culture-pdf-d219931240

10   Hofstede, G. (n.d.). Geert Hofstede. Retrieved from http://www.geerthofstede.nl

11   Willems, A., De Ruyck, T. & Schillewaert, N. (2013). What Happens if Community Members Start Acting as Researchers. Quirk's Magazine.

12   Van den Bergh, J. & Behrer, M. (2011). How Cool Brands Stay Hot: Branding to Generation Y. London: Kogan Page.

13   Van den Bergh, J. & Boullart, A. (2013). No guts, no glory: 5 steps to become a brave new mar-
      keter. InSites Consulting Publication.

14   Van den Bergh, J. et al. (2012). How to connect with urban Millennials: Engaging Gen Yers from
      15 global cities to understand drivers of cool places, products and brands. InSites Consulting
      Publication.

15   Greenbook Research Industry Trends Report (2013). Retrieved from http://www.greenbookblog.org/grit

Chapter 5: Shaping the future together

1   LeDoux, J. (1998). The emotional brain: the mysterious underpinnings of emotional life. New York:
     Simon & Schuster Inc.

2   Verhaeghe, A. et al. (2010). Synergizing natural and research communities: Caring about the
     research ecosystem. ESOMAR Online Research Congress.

3   Rix J. (2013). The Insumer. Research Live. Retrieved from http://www.research-live.com/features/
     the-insumer/4009533.article

4   Troch, T. et al. (2012). Walking the talk: co-creating the future of market research online communi-
     ties. International Journal of Market Research, 54(4), 570–572.

5   De Ruyck, T. et al. (2011). Engage, Inspire, Act: 3 Step Stones towards Developing more
     Impactful Products. ESOMAR General Congress.

6   De Ruyck, T. et al. (2012). Designing the Club of Tomorrow: Consumer Understanding Guiding
     Creativity towards Success. ESOMAR General Congress.

7   Troch, T. et al. (2012). Doing More with Less: Crossing the Boundaries of Qualitative to Increase
     Business Impact. ESOMAR Qualitative Congress.

The basics of Consumer Consulting Boards

1   Greenbook Research Industry Trends Report. (2013). Retrieved from http://www.greenbookblog.org/grit

2   Van Belleghem, S., De Ruyck, T. & Thijs, D. (2012). Social Media around the World. InSites
     Consulting Publication.

3   Van Belleghem, S., De Ruyck, T. & Thijs, D. (2012). Social Media around the World. InSites
     Consulting Publication.